SURVIVAL
TAGALOG

How to communicate without fuss or fear INSTANTLY!

SECOND EDITION

by JOI BARRIOS

T0354034

TUTTLE Publishing

Tokyo | Rutland, Vermont | Singapore

CONTENTS

PART 2
Numbers and Counting

PART 3
Let's see/eat/do everything!

PART 4
Geography Guide & Reading Signs

PART 5
Additional Vocabulary

TAGALOG, PILIPINO, OR FILIPINO?

Is the Tagalog language different from the Filipino language? What is Pilipino? What language is being taught in this book?

The Tagalog People, the Language and Philippine History

The word *Tagalog* refers to an ethnolinguistic group—the Tagalog, as well as their language. It is derived from the word **taga-ilog**, meaning "from the river." The Tagalog is one of the largest ethnolinguistic groups in the Philippines, and they were the indigenous inhabitants of several provinces in Luzon, among them, Rizal, Bulacan, Laguna, Nueva Ecija, Quezon, and what is now known as the capital center, Metro Manila.

To understand the answer to "what language are we learning here, anyway?" a short history lesson will help. The Philippines was occupied by three main colonial powers: Spain (1565–1898); the United States (1899–1942); and the Japanese (1942–1945).* Several expeditions by the Spaniards in the 16th century led to their colonization of the islands which they named Las Islas Filipinas, after Spain's King Felipe II. In spite of initial resistance and sporadic peasant revolts, Spain ruled the country for three hundred years, defeated only through the Philippine revolution of 1896. Independence was declared on June 12, 1898, but was short-lived.

* Britain declared war against Spain in 1762, and Manila was captured by the British. With the signing of the "Peace of Paris," in 1763, the British left Manila the following year, and Spain continued its colonial rule of the islands.

On December 10 of that same year, the Treaty of Paris was signed by two nations at war—Spain and the United States, and the Philippine delegate was excluded from the sessions and negotiations. Among the provisions of the treaty was the surrender of the Philippines to the United States for the sum of twenty million dollars. The occupation of the islands by the new colonial power was met with strong resistance, resulting in the Philippine-American War (also known as the Philippine War of Independence) from 1899 to 1902. It was only in 1935 that a Commonwealth government was established following several independence missions to the United States. And only in 1946, after Japanese occupation during World War II, did the Philippines become an independent nation.

How did the colonial experience affect the language? In three ways—vocabulary, language policy, and orthography or letters.

Vocabulary

Let us first look into vocabulary. When you listen to Filipinos speak to one another, you may be able to understand a few words here and there. That's because many words are derived from Spanish and English. For example, words such as **mesa** (Spanish—*mesa*; English—table), **kabayo** (Spanish—*caballo*; English—horse), and **sarswela** (Spanish—*zarzuela*, a type of play with music) are words that represent the dominance of the colonial culture introduced by the Spaniards. Similarly, words such as **taksi** (taxi), **hamburger**, and **Amerikana** (referring to suits worn by men) are used, either retaining the English spelling (**hamburger**) or using a Filipino one (**taksi**), or by giving a new meaning to the word (**Amerikana**).

You may also know of the term "Taglish" or "Tagalog English," which refers to code-switching, or the shifting from one language to another mid-sentence or mid-conversation. For example, while shopping, a Filipino might ask a sales clerk: "Excuse me, **magkano po ang blouse na ito?** Can I see **iyong** gray blouse?" (Excuse me, how much is this blouse? Can I see the gray blouse?)

Also, many recent words brought about by technology, such as "computer," "flight," and "x-ray," obviously have no indigenous equivalents, so are just used as they are. As a learner, you should feel comfortable just using these words instead of looking for equivalents which you will probably not find in a dictionary anyway.

Language Policy

You may be curious as to why many Filipinos choose to speak in English or in Taglish, and why those coming from old, affluent families speak Spanish. The colonial experience affected language policies, and during the Spanish colonial period, Spanish was the official language used for documents, communications and courts, and was considered to be the language only of the elite and the educated.

During the American colonial rule, both Spanish and English were the official languages, and English became the medium of instruction. In 1935, with the installation of the Commonwealth government, then-President Manuel Quezon established the Surian ng Wikang Pambansa (Institute of National Language). It was the Surian that chose Tagalog as the basis for the national language in 1937; and in 1959, the Department of Education issued a memorandum that specified for the teaching of a national language called Pilipino.

Language policy changed again in 1973, a year after martial law was declared by President Ferdinand Marcos, and both Pilipino and English became the official languages of the country. With the ousting of Marcos in 1986 through what is now called the "People Power revolt" and with the promulgation of a new constitution in 1987 came yet another change. The national language became known as Filipino.

According to Article XIV, Section 6 of the 1987 constitution: "The national language of the Philippines is Filipino. As it evolves, it shall be further developed and enriched on the basis of existing Philippine and other languages."

This meant that no longer shall Tagalog be the only basis for the language called Filipino, but *other* Philippine languages shall be as well. How many other Philippine languages are there? According to the Komisyon sa Wikang Filipino (Commission on the Filipino Languages) there are 175 indigenous languages, four of which have no known speakers.

Orthography

This brings us now to the changes in the letters of Tagalog/Pilipino/Filipino. While Tagalog has twenty letters (*a, b, k, d, e, g, h, i, l, m, n, ng, o, p, r, s, t, u, w* and *y*), Filipino has 8 more (*c, f, j, ñ, q, v, x, z*). These letters are not only found in the Spanish and English languages—the Cordillera language has *f*, the Ibanag has *v*, and Ivatan has *f*.

Let me give a few examples. Should you, by chance, encounter Tagalog documents written or published in the 18th or 19th centuries, you will notice that Spanish letters were used then—thus letters such as *k* and *w* were not used. For example, what is now spelled as **kapantay** (meaning "equal")

was spelled *capantay*, and what is now spelled as **malinaw**
(meaning "clear") was spelled *malinao*. However, in 1935, the
letters *k* and *w* were added to the alphabet by the government,
so *capantay* became **kapantay**, and *malinao* became **malinaw**. Today, some people would retain the original spelling
of the word "computer"; others would spell it "**kompyuter**,"
using the letter *k*.

What language are you learning in this book? This is how I
would explain it—we are using Filipino the national language,
that is primarily based on the Tagalog language. We are studying the everyday language of the political and business center
Metro Manila.

So it doesn't matter if you say, "**Nag-aaral ako ng Tagalog/
Pilipino/Filipino**." (I study Tagalog/Pilipino/Filipino.) And
even if you forget the verb "**aral**" (study) and say, "**Nagsa**study
ako ng Tagalog/Pilipino/Filipino," there is no language police. Just speak the language the best that you can!

INTRODUCTION

A, B, C ... the Tagalog and Filipino Alphabets

The Tagalog language has only twenty letters, *a, b, k, d, e, g, h, i, l, m, n, ng, o, p, r, s, t, u, w* and *y*. However, the Filipino language, as it is used today, has 28, because of the addition of 8 letters, *c, f, j, ñ, q, v, x,* and *n*.

The Unfamiliar Letters Ñ and Ng

Two letters in the alphabet may be unfamiliar to you.

First, **ñ**—this is the Spanish *ñ*. Pronounce it the way it is pronounced in Spanish. For example, the word for *pineapple* is **piña**, also spelled as **pinya**.

When spelled with an *ñ*, it is pronounced *PIN-ya*, with the accent on the first syllable (approximating a more "Spanish" sound).

When spelled with the letters *n* and *y*, **pinya**, it is pronounced *pi-NYA*, with the accent on the second syllable.

You will find that in most cases, the spelling and pronunciation has been adapted to Filipino/Tagalog, but you can still find the letter *ñ* used in names and in other words.

Second, the letter **ng** may be pronounced as "*nang*" when used alone as a word, or pronounced as a singular sound "*ng*" when it occurs at the end of a word (for example, **lutang**, pronounced *lu-tang*, meaning "float") or when it's followed by a vowel (for example, **sanga**, pronounced *sa-NGA*, accent on the second syllable, meaning "branch").

See It, Say It: Pronunciation Guidelines & Tips

For Filipino/Tagalog, we read a word the way it is spelled, and we spell it the way we read. There are no long vowel sounds.

Basic Sounds

Let us pair off the letter *b* with the vowel *a*. Remember the language only has short vowel sounds...no long vowels, no extended vowels, and no aspirated sounds.

Now practice saying these syllables:

ba	**be**	**bi**	**bo**	**bu**

To guide you, here are some words as well as comparisons to sounds in the English language. Note that the accents in the vowels indicate that the stress is on the first syllable.

ba in **báyad** (payment) with the **ba** close to the **a** in "baccarat" (card game)

be in **bénda** (bandage) with the **be** close to the **be** in "bend"

bi in **bíbe** (duck) with the **bi** close to "bee" (the insect)

bo in **bóte** (bottle) with the **bo** close to "bought"

bu in **búkas** (tomorrow) with the **bu** in "boom"

Now try it with the other letters:

ka	**ke**	**ki**	**ko**	**ku**
da	**de**	**di**	**do**	**du**
ga	**ge**	**gi**	**go**	**gu**

ha	he	hi	ho	hu
la	le	li	lo	lu
ma	me	me	mo	mu
na	ne	ni	no	nu
pa	pe	pi	po	pu
ra	re	ri	ro	ru
sa	se	si	so	su
ta	te	ti	to	tu
wa	we	wi	wo	wu
ya	ye	yi	yo	yu

Diphthongs

There are five Tagalog diphthongs (groups of letters that make a single sound): *iw, ay, aw, oy,* and *uy.* When you see these, remember that the pronunciation is very different from the way you would pronounce it in English.

For example:

DIPHTHONG	WORD	MEANING
ay	**lamay**	funeral wake
	("la" "my")	

With the accent on the first syllable, pronounce the second syllable like English word "my." Do not pronounce it the way the word "may" (meaning "can") is pronounced in English.

Another example is the diphthong *aw*:

DIPHTHONG	WORD	MEANING
aw	**bataw**	bean pod

With the accent on the first syllable, pronounce the *aw* here in a way close to the sound *taw* in the English word "towel." Don't pronounce it the way you would the English word "raw."

Similarly, the three other diphthongs are pronounced the same way. Try them:

	WORD	MEANING
iw	**aliw**	fun (accent on the second syllable)
oy	**kumunoy**	quicksand (accent on the third syllable). This is similar to the sound in the English word "an*noy*."
uy	**kasuy**	cashew

Two Vowels but Not Diphthongs

You may also find some words with two vowels together that are not diphthongs, but which you may mistake for such—if English is your native language, then you might naturally tend to read these as diphthongs (or as letters with a single sound). Instead, pronounce them as the separate sounds they are. For example:

	WORD		MEANING
ae	**babae**	pronounced *ba-ba-e*	woman
ai	**mabait**	pronounced *ma-ba-it*	good person
	kain	pronounced *ka-in*	to eat
ao	**baon**	pronounced *ba-on*	something you bring when you travel

Thus, when you see these vowels together, you simply need to break the word into syllables.

Understanding Interchangeable Letters and Sounds

As you learn the language and listen to native speakers, you might find something puzzling—people interchange the letters *d* and *r*, and the vowels *e* and *i*, and *o* and *u*.

For example, some people say **madami** (many); others will say **marami**. People may say either **lalaki** or **lalake** (man) and either **babae** or **babai** (pronounced *ba-ba-e*) (woman).

Why is this so? This may be because in the ancient Tagalog script, the **baybayin**, there was only one symbol for *d/r*, and for *e/i* and *o/u*.*

Today, with the standardization of spelling and grammatical rules, there are guidelines now for the use of *d/r*. However, you will find that when Filipinos speak, they are less conscious of the rules and will interchange, for example, the word **daw** (also) with **raw**. Similarly, the words **babae** (woman) and **lalaki** (man) each have that standardized spelling; however, in spoken Filipino the *e/i* sounds are interchangeable for these words.

Stresses

Now let's turn to stresses: what syllable should you emphasize when you say a word? Tagalog language books used to actually show printed stress marks, but now, if you read newspapers or literature, no stress marks can be found. Here are some important points to remember:

---

* In recent years, you may find that many Filipino-Americans, Filipino Canadians or those born in other countries who are of Filipino descent have studied the **baybayin** as a way of learning more about their heritage. There are websites such as www.baybayin.com and www.eaglescorner.com/baybayin/baybayin.html which you may want to explore.

1. For most words with three or four syllables, the stress is usually on the second to the last syllable. Some examples are: Tagalog, Pilipino, **ba<u>ba</u>e** (woman), **la<u>la</u>ki** (man), **ka-<u>ba</u>taan**.

2. Sometimes a vowel is said with a glottal sound—produced by closing your throat abruptly. For example: **batì** (greeting), **<u>ta</u>ma** (prediction), **pa<u>y</u>apà** (peaceful). In some of the words in this book, this glottal sound will be indicted by the grave accent mark (`` ` ``). Remember, the mark means "glottal sound"—it does not mean to stress that syllable.

3. In many pronunciation guides, you will find the symbol ^ above the vowel of the last syllable. This means two things: the accent is on the last syllable; and there is a glottal stop on the vowel. Some examples are: **dagâ** (mouse), **ba-hâ**, (flood), **walâ** (don't have; nothing) and **hindî** (no).

4. Sometimes the stress is on the last syllable. Some examples are: **da<u>sál</u>** (prayer), **kumus<u>tá</u>** (how are you?) and **ka<u>yó</u>** (second person plural pronoun). In some of the words in this book, this will be indicated by the acute stress mark (´).

5. Some long words (with three or four syllables) have an additional stress. Two examples are **eskuwélahán** (school) and **mágnanakáw** (thief).

6. Accents and stress can be confusing when words are put together. For example, when the word **ako** (I or me) is used alone, the accent is clearly on the second syllable (*a-kó*). When used with the word **po** (honorific) to show respect, as in the phrase **Ako po si Kathleen**, native speakers seem to say "**ako po**" as if they were one word (*a-ko-po*) with the accent on the syllable **po**.

Dictionary Guides versus Spoken Filipino

Sometimes, dictionaries will syllabicate words differently than what you may hear/perceive to hear when native speakers speak. Two examples are the word **siya** (third person singular pronoun) and **Biyernes** (Friday).

In most dictionary entries, **siya** will appear as "*si-ya*" and you will understand this to mean that there are two syllables, "*si*" and "*ya*." However, when you hear a native speaker ask the question "**Sino siya?**" (Who is she/he?), you hear "*Si-no sha?*" Which, then, is the correct pronunciation? Both are correct. The sound "*sha*" is simply a fast way of saying **siya** thus making it seem like one syllable.

Similarly, **Biyernes** is seen as "*Bi-yer-nes*" but can be pronounced "*Byer-nes*."

For this guide, I opted for the traditional way—"*si-ya*" and "*Bi-yer-nes*." Why? Because it is easier to learn the language if you learn these syllables. However, as you get more accustomed to it, you can speak these words faster and sound like a native speaker!

Summing Up

Here are some key pronunciation tips, some of which reiterate what we've discussed:

1. There are no long vowel sounds in Filipino/Tagalog. Do not extend the sound of the vowel. For example, when saying "**Kumusta ka?**" (How are you?), do not say "*Kumusta kaaaaaaa?*"

2. Unless you are asking a question, the intonation should fall at the end of the sentence.

3. When you see two vowels together, bear in mind that they are not pronounced as one vowel.

4. Some letters such as *d/r*, *i/e* and *o/u* may be pronounced interchangeably by some speakers.

5. Practice the diphthongs discussed on pages 12–13. When you look at the pronunciation guide that appears after each sentence in this guide, if you see **hay** (as in **buhay** or life), remember that this is pronounced like *high*.

6. In many instances, you will hear that pronunciation varies. So if you hear someone say *ba-ba-e* and another say *ba-ba-i*, that is fine. Also, **siya** (third person pronoun, singular) will sometimes be pronounced *si-ya* (the official dictionary pronunciation), while you may hear other people pronounce this as *sha* with a noticeable *h* sound.

7. In this book, diacritic marks will only appear when a word has to be said quickly and the accent is on the last syllable; when there is a glottal stop; and to avoid confusion in case the accent changes the meaning of a word. Moreover, the accent only appears the first time the word is used.

8. To review: **báyad** (noun, payment) shows that the accent is on the first syllable; **bayád** (has been paid [verb]) shows that the accent is on the last syllable; **tamà** (correct) shows that there is a glottal sound and the accent is on the first syllable; and **hindî** (no) shows that there is a glottal stop and the accent is on the second syllable.

Get Sentenced! Grammar

I usually advise students to learn three things: how affixes change words; honorifics or words used for polite language such as **po** and **opo**; and the structure of the language—and then just to plunge into speaking the language. For example, let's say you know of the affix **nag-**. Now, a friend asks you "**Ano ang ginagawa mo tuwing Sabado?**" (What do you do on Saturdays?). If you play soccer, you can just say, "**Nagsa-soccer ako.**" (I [play] soccer.) Note that the affix **nag** was simply added to the word *soccer* and the first syllable of soccer ("*sa*") was just repeated.

Some students of mine will just add "**po**" to every sentence to "sound Filipino" to their parents.

Parent: What time will you be home?
Student: I don't know **po**.

There are four main points we need to remember in Tagalog/Filipino grammar: sentence order; focus and markers; the complex system of affixes; and aspects of the verb.

1. In spoken Filipino, the usual order of the sentence is verb-subject-object.

    In English we say: *I am eating an apple.*

    In Tagalog/Filipino, we say: *Eating I* marker *apple.*
    (**Kumakain ako *ng* mansanas.**)

    The marker here is **ng** because it "marks" the object—the apple.

2. This bring us to the second point: markers, focus and affixes. Tagalog/Filipino has a complex system of affixes and these affixes change depending on the focus of the sentence. For example:

Kumain *si* John ng mansanas.
John ate an apple.
(Literally, Ate *marker* John *marker* apple.)

The focus here is on John as indicated by the marker **si**, and not on the apple he is eating.

If we would like to change this and make the apple (**mansanas**) the focus instead of John, the doer of the action, then we can say:

Mansanas *ang* kinain ni John.
Apple is what John ate.
(Literally, Apple *marker* eating *marker* John.)

We know that the focus is on the apple because of the marker **ang** which is closer to the word **mansanas** (apple).

3. Third, as you may have noticed by now, the affix used for the verb **kain** (to eat) changes depending on the focus.

When the focus was on the subject or the doer of the action we used **um** before the first vowel of the root word **kain**. Thus "**um**" + "**kain**" results in **kumain**. When the focus was on the object "apple," we used the affix **in** before the first vowel of the root word **kain**. Thus, "**in**" + "**kain**" results in **kinain**.

As you read and speak Tagalog/Filipino, a good knowledge of affixes will be helpful. Let us go back to our root word **kain** or "eat."

With the affix:

- **pag** → "**pagkain**." The affix **pag**, usually used for nouns, gives us a clue that "**pagkain**" means "food."

- **nagpa** → "**nagpakain**," and means you did something for others. "**Nagpakain ako sa mga kaibigan ko.**" (I fed or gave food to my friends.)

- **pina** → "**pinakain**," and means someone did something for you. "**Pinakain ako ng kaibigan ko.**" (My friend fed or gave food to me.)

- **pa** → "**pakain**," which you use when asking a favor. "**Pakain!**" (Please let me eat some of the food you have.)

Some affixes also give you clues to the meaning of words. The affix **ka**, for example, connotes relationships. A few words that start with **ka** are **kapatid** (brother/sister), **kaibigan** (friend) and **kaklase** (classmate).

The affix **ma** is usually used for adjectives: **mabait** (good person), **maganda** (beautiful), **matangkad** (tall person).

4. Finally, most Filipino language scholars are of the opinion that Tagalog/Filipino does not have tenses, but aspects. Instead of past, present, and future tenses, Tagalog/Filipino has completed, incompleted, and contemplated aspects.

Completed action—**Kumain ako ng mansanas.**
(*I ate an apple.*) (literally, Ate I *marker* apple.)

Incompleted action—**Kumakain ako ng mansanas.**
(*I am eating an apple.*) (literally, Eating I *marker* apple.)

Contemplated action—**Kakain ako ng mansanas.**
(*I will eat an apple.*) (literally, Will eat I *marker* apple.)

For the equivalent of the present perfect tense, simply add the word **na**.

For example, in response to the question, "Have you eaten?" we can answer: **Kumain na ako.** (*I have eaten.*) (literally, Eaten already I.)

Or in response to the question "Have you ever eaten an apple?" we can use the affix **naka-**: *Naka*kain **na ako ng mansanas.** (*I have eaten apples.*) (literally, Have eaten already I *marker* apple.) Here the verb is used with the affix **naka**, connoting "have eaten."

Many people tend to be overwhelmed by all these grammar rules. But this is what I think: your goal is not to have the most perfect grammar. It is to use the language to communicate. Remember that most Filipinos will not mind a grammar slip here and there…so just start speaking!

PART ONE

Common Expressions and Key Words

HI! GOODBYE! GREETINGS

The Philippines	***Pilipínas*** *(Pi-li-pí-nas)/* ***Filipinas*** *(Fi-li-pí-nas)*
Republika ng Filipinas	***Republika ng Pilipinas*** *(Re-pub-li-ká nang Pi-li-pi-nas)*
the Tagalog language	***Tagalog*** *(Ta-gá-log)*
Filipino language	***Filipino/Pilipino*** *(Fi-li-pí-no/Ta-gá-log)*
Filipino men	***Filipino/Pilipino*** *(Fi-li-pí-no/Pi-li-pí-no)*
Filipino women	***Filipina/Pilipina*** *(Fi-li-pí-na/Pi-li-pí-no)*
Filipino American	***Filipino Amerikano*** *(Fi-li-pí-no A-me-ri-ká-no)*
Manila	***Maynila*** *(May-ni-là)*

Here are some common greetings and responses:

▶ **How are you?**
   Kumusta ka?
   (Ku-mus-tà ka)

▶ **I'm fine. Thank you.**
   Mabuti. Salamat.
   (Ma-bu-ti. Sa-la-mat)

▶ **I'm okay.**
   Okay lang.
   (O-kay lang)

It is not unusual to use Miss, Mister, Mrs. and Ms. with surnames. However, we have included here their equivalents in Filipino/Tagalog in case you may hear these words spoken in the country. Also, know that Filipinos have a fondness for titles. For example, professionals are usually addressed in this manner: "Doctor Lumbera," "Engineer Icasiano," or "Attorney Taguiwalo."

▶ **Good morning, Mr. Cruz!**
   Magandang umaga, Ginoong Cruz!
   (Ma-gan-dáng u-ma-ga, Gi-no-ong Cruz)

▶ **Good afternoon, Mrs. Santos!**
   Magandang hapon, Ginang Santos!
   (Ma-gan-dáng ha-pon, Gi-nang San-tos)

▶ **Good evening, Miss Pineda!**
   Magandang gabi, Binibining Pineda!
   (Ma-gan-dáng ga-bi, Bi-ni-bi-ning Pineda)

When you are visiting a friend's house, knocking or using the doorbell, and would like to signify your presence:

▶ **I am here!**
   Tao po! (literally, there is a person here!)
   (Ta-o po)

▶ **Please come in!**
   Tuloy po kayo!
   (Tu-loy po ka-yó)

To be more polite, use the honorifics "**po**" and "**ho**" and the second person plural "**kayo**" instead of "**ka.**" For example, when addressing an older person, say:

▶ **How are you?**
   Kumusta po kayo?
   (Ku-mus-ta po ka-yó)

▶ **I'm fine. Thank you.**
Mabuti po. Salamat.
(Ma-bu-ti po. Sa-la-mat)

▶ **Good morning!**
Magandang umaga po!
(Ma-gan-dáng u-ma-ga po)

When meeting each other on the street, Filipinos also like to ask each other where they have been or where they are going. This is not to be interpreted as nosiness, but just as a common way of greeting.

▶ **Where did you come from?**
Saan ka galing?
(Sa-án ka gá-ling)

   Saan po kayo galing? (formal)
   (Sa-án po ka-yó ga-ling)

▶ **I came from my house.**
Galing ako sa bahay ko.
(Ga-ling a-kó sa ba-hay ko)

   Galing po ako sa bahay ko. (formal)
   (Ga-ling po a-kó sa ba-hay ko)

► **I came from __** (insert place).
Galing ako sa __.
(Ga-ling a-kó sa __)

► **Where are you going?**
Saan ka pupunta?
(Sa-án ka pu-pun-ta)

Saan po kayo pupunta? (formal)
(Sa-án po ka-yó pu-pun-ta)

► **I am going to ___.**
Pupunta ako sa __.
(Pú-pun-ta a-kó sa__)

In these next common greetings/sentences, the formal form is used because most of the situations are interactions with strangers. Also, it is better to err on the side of "politeness." In some cases, both the formal and informal phrases are given. When you are speaking to someone familiar to you and/or of the same age simply omit the word "**po**."

► **Do you speak English?**
Marunong po ba kayong mag-Ingles? (formal)
(Ma-ru-nong po ba ka-yóng mag-Ing-gles)

▶ **I understand.**
Naiintindihan ko po.
(Na-í-in-tín-di-hán ko po)

▶ **I don't understand.**
Hindi ko po naiintindihan.
(Hin-dî ko po na-í-in-tín-di-hán)

▶ **Can you speak slowly please?**
Pakibagalan po ninyo ang pagsasalita. (formal)
(Pa-kí-ba-gá-lan po nin-yo ang pág-sa-sá-li-tâ)

▶ **Please write it down.**
Pakisulat po.
(Pa-ki-su-lat po)

▶ **What is this called in Tagalog/Filipino?**
Ano po ang tawag dito sa Tagalog/Filipino?
(A-no po ang ta-wag di-to sa Ta-ga-log/Fi-li-pi-no)

GOODBYE

Paalam. (most formal)
(Pa-a-lam)

Sige. (literally, okay)
(Si-ge)

▶ **Let us see each other again.**
Magkita po tayo ulit.
(Mag-ki-ta po ta-yo u-lit)

▶ **Until then…**
Hanggang sa muli po…
(Hang-gáng sa mu-li po)

▶ **Until we meet again.**
Hanggang sa susunod na pagkikita.
(Hang-gáng sa sú-su-nod na pag-ki-ki-ta)

Also, people tend to ask each other to be careful when saying goodbye:

▶ **Be careful.**
Mag-ingat po kayo.
(Mag-i-ngat po ka-yó)

▶ **Thank you.**
Salamat po.
(Sa-la-mat po)

▶ **Thank you very much.**
Maraming salamat po.
(Ma-ra-ming sa-la-mat po)

► **Thank you too.**
Maraming salamat din po.
(Ma-ra-ming sa-la-mat din po)

► **You are welcome.**
Walang anuman po.
(Wa-láng a-nu-man po)

PARDON ME...

There are many ways to say "excuse me," depending on the situation, and many ways to apologize, ranging from the most informal to the most formal.

► **Excuse me...**
Mawalang galang na po... (formal, used to begin a question or when interrupting someone)
(Ma-wa-láng ga-lang na po)

► **Excuse me (please let me pass)...**
Makikiraan po...
(Ma-kí-ki-ra-án po)

► **I am sorry.**
Pasensiya ka na.
(Pa-sen-s-ya ka na)

Pasensiya na po kayo. (formal)
(Pa-sen-s-ya na po ka-yó)

► **Please forgive me.**
Patawarin mo ako. *(Pa-ta-wa-rin mo a-kó)*

Patawad. (used only in very formal situations)
(Pa-ta-wad)

► **I did not mean (to do it).**
Hindi ko sinasadya.
(Hin-dî ko si-ná-sad-yâ)

► **May I disturb you...**
Maabala ko po kayo... (used when asking a favor
of someone who is at work)
(Ma-a-ba-la ko po ka-yó)

► **Sorry I disturbed you.**
Pasensiya na at naabala ko kayo.
(Pa-sen-si-ya na at na-a-ba-la ko ka-yó)

ON THE PHONE

When you're talking on the phone, these are some
useful phrases and sentences:

► **Hello?**
   Hello.
   (He-lo)

► **This is ___ (name).**
   Si __ po ito.
   (Si __ po i-tó)

► **Who would you like to speak to?**
   Sino po ang gusto ninyong makausap?
   (Si-no po ang gus-to nin-yóng ma-ka-u-sap)

► **One moment please.**
   Sandali lang po.
   (San-da-lî lang po)

► **Yes, that's right.**
   Opo, tama po.
   (O-po, ta-ma po)

► **He/she is not here.**
   Wala po siya rito.
   (Wa-la po si-ya ri-to)

► **You have the wrong number.**
   Mali po yata ang numero ninyo.
   (literally, Perhaps your number is wrong.)
   (Ma-li po yâ-ta ang nu-me-ro nin-yó)

CHATTING

To talk about what you do or what you're doing in the
Philippines, you can say:

▶ **I'm here on business.**
May trabaho po ako rito.
(literally, I have a job here.)
(May tra-ba-ho po a-kó ri-to)

May negosyo po ako rito.
(literally, I have a business here.)
(May ne-gos-yo po a-kó ri-to)

▶ **I'm studying here.**
Nag-aaral po ako rito.
(Nag-a-a-ral po a-kó ri-to)

▶ **I'm a tourist.**
Turista po ako.
(Tu-ris-ta po a-kó)

▶ **I'm visiting friends.**
Binibisita ko po ang mga kaibigan ko.
(Bi-ní-bi-sí-ta ko po ang ma-nga ka-i-bi-gan ko)

To talk about conditions/feelings:

▶ **I'm tired.**
   Pagod po ako.
   (Pa-god po a-kó)

▶ **I'm sick.**
   May sakit po ako.
   (May sa-kít po a-kó)

▶ **I feel sick.**
   Masama po ang pakiramdam ko.
   (Ma-sa-ma po ang pa-ki-ram-dám ko)

▶ **I have a cold.**
   May sipon po ako.
   (May si-pón po a-kó)

▶ **I'm hungry.**
   Nagugutom po ako.
   (Na-gu-gu-tom po a-kó)

▶ **I'm thirsty.**
   Nauuhaw po ako.
   (Na-u-u-haw po a-kó)

Here are what I like to call useful "reaction shots." These are common expressions you can try with your friends.

► **Really?**
Talaga?
(Ta-la-ga)

► **Is that so?**
Ganoon ba?
(Ga-no-on ba)

► **That's true.**
Totoo 'yan.
(To-to-o yan)

► **That's good!**
Mabuti naman.
(Ma-bu-ti na-man)

► **What a pity!**
Sayang!
(Sa-yang)

► **Poor you!**
Kawawa ka naman.
(Ka-wa-wa ka na-man)

("**Kawawa**" is a favorite expression of many… to indicate sympathy.)

▶ **Poor ___ (name)!**
Kawawa naman si __ !
(Ka-wa-wa na-man si __)

I'M MELISSA. YOU'RE SAM. WHO'S HE? PERSONAL THINGS

Remember that there are two sets of pronouns for I, you, and he/she, depending on the focus of the sentence: either on the subject or doer of the action, or on the object. When talking to strangers or older people, we use the second person plural. Again, here I am assuming that you are talking to a stranger, so the honorific **po** is used. When talking to people who are familiar to you, or of the same age, simply omit the "**po**."

(Pronunciation note: As on page 17, point no. 7, the focus of the pronunciation guidelines is on syllabication. Stress guidelines for the new words can be found in the boxes containing them. However, some stresses also appear in cases when there might be confusion.

I   ***ako*** *(a-kó)*, ***ko*** *(ko)*

▶ **I am Melissa.**
Ako po si Melissa.
(A-ko po si Me-li-sa)

► **I am ___ (name).**
  Ako po si ___ .
  (A-ko po si ___)

► **I'm from Los Angeles.**
  Taga-Los Angeles po ako.
  (Ta-gá Los Angeles po a-ko)

► **I'm from ___ (place).**
  Taga-___ po ako.
  (Ta-gá-___ po a-ko)

► **I live in Manila.**
  Nakatira po ako sa Maynila.
  (Na-ka-ti-ra po a-ko sa May-ni-la)

► **I'm an engineer.**
  Inhinyero po ako./Engineer po ako.
  (In-hin-ye-ro po a-ko./En-gi-neer po a-ko)

► **I'm a doctor.**
  Doktor po ako./Doktora po ako. (said by female
  speaker)
  (Dok-tór po a-kó/Dok-to-ra po a-ko)
  (Note: Women can use either "**doktor**" or "**doktora**.")

► **I'm a student.**
  Estudyante po ako.
  (Es-tud-yan-te po a-ko)

▶ **I'm retired.**
Retirado na po ako.
(Re-ti-ra-do na po a-ko)

▶ **I don't know.**
Hindi ko po alam.
(Hin-dî ko po a-lam)

▶ **I think so.**
Sa tingin ko po.
(Sa ti-ngín ko po)

▶ **I am going.**
Pupunta po ako.
(Pu-pun-ta po a-ko)

▶ **I am not going.**
Hindi po ako pupunta.
(Hin-dî po a-ko pu-pun-ta)

▶ **I would like to go.**
Gusto kong pumunta.
(Gus-to kong pu-mun-tá)

Gusto ko pong pumunta. (formal)
(Gus-to ko pong pu-mun-tá)

▶ **I would like to go to Roxas Avenue.**
Gusto ko pong pumunta sa Roxas Avenue.
(Gus-to ko pong pu-mun-tá sa Ro-has A-ven-yu)

▶ **Can I take a picture of you?**
Puwede ko po ba kayong kunan ng larawan?
(Pwe-de ko po ba ka-yong kunan nang la-ra-wan)

▶ **Can you take a picture of us?**
Puwede po ba ninyo kaming kunan ng larawan?
(Pwe-de po ba nin-yo ka-ming ku-nan nang la-ra-wan)

▶ **Please give me a glass of water.**
Pakibigyan po ninyo ako ng isang basong tubig.
(Pa-ki-big-yan po nin-yo a-ko nang i-sang ba-song tu-big)

▶ **Can I ask for water?**
Puwede po bang humingi ng tubig?
(Pwe-de po bang hu-mi-ngi nang tu-big)

My **ko** *(ko)*

▶ **Where is my room?**
Saan po ang kuwarto ko?
(Sa-án po ang kwar-to ko)

► **Here is my address.**
Heto po ang tirahan ko.
(He-to po ang ti-ra-han ko)

► **This is my bag.**
Bag ko po ito.
(Bag ko po i-tó)

Mine   *akin (a-kin)*

► **This bag is mine.**
Akin ang bag na ito.
(A-kin ang bag na i-tó)

You   *ikaw (i-kaw), ka (ka),*
                kayo (formal) (ka-yo)

► **You are Pierre.**
Ikaw si Pierre./Si Pierre ka.
(I-kaw si Pierre/Si Pierre ka)

► **You are Mr. Santos.**
Kayo po si Mr. Santos.
(Ka-yo po si Mr. San-tos)

    Si Mr. Santos po kayo. (formal)
    (Si Mis-ter San-tos po ka-yó)

▶ **Where are you from?**
Taga-saan po kayo?
(Ta-gá-sa-án po ka-yó)

▶ **Where do you live?**
Saan po kayo nakatira?
(Sa-án po ka-yó na-ká-ti-rá)

Your .*mo (mo)*, ***ninyo** (nin-yó)* (formal)

▶ **Is this your umbrella?**
Payong po ba ninyo ito?
(Pa-yong po ba nin-yó i-to)

He/She *siya (si-yá)*
(sometimes pronounced as *sya*)

▶ **Who is he/she?**
Sino po siya?
(Si-no po si-ya)

▶ **Is he/she a doctor?**
Doktor/Doktora po ba siya?
(Dok-tór/Dok-to-ra po ba si-ya)

▶ **He/she is my friend.**
Kaibigan ko po siya.
(Ka-i-bi-gan ko po si-ya)

▶ **He/she is not here.**
Wala po siya rito.
(Wa-la po si-ya ri-to)

His/Her   *niya (ni-ya)*
              (sometimes pronounced as *nya*)

▶ **That is his/her book.**
Libro po niya iyan.
(Lib-ró po ni-ya i-yan)
(Note: Sometimes *iyan* is pronounced as *'yan*.)

His/Hers   *kanya (kan-yá)*

▶ **That book is his/hers.**
Kanya po ang libro na iyan.
(Kan-ya po ang lib-ro na i-yan)

Him/Her   *kanya (kan-ya)*

▶ **Give the book to him/her.**
   Ibigay mo ang libro sa kanya.
   (I-bi-gay mo ang lib-ro sa kan-ya)

▶ **Please give the book to him/her.**
   Pakibigay mo ang libro sa kanya.
   (Pa-ki-bi-gay mo ang lib-ro sa kan-ya)

Name   *pangalan (pa-nga-lan)*

▶ **What is your name?**
   Ano ang pangalan mo?
   (A-nó ang pa-nga-lan mo)

   Ano po ang pangalan ninyo? (formal)
   (A-no po ang pa-nga-lan nin-yó)

▶ **My name is Melissa.**
   Melissa po ang pangalan ko.
   (Me-li-sa po ang pa-nga-lan ko)

▶ **What is his/her name?**
   Ano po ang pangalan niya?
   (A-no po ang pa-nga-lan ni-ya)

Family Name   *apelyido (a-pel-yi-do)*

▶ **What is your family name?**
Ano po ang apelyido ninyo?
(A-no po ang a-pel-yi-do nin-yo)

▶ **My family name is Yengko.**
Yengko po ang apelyido ko.
(Yeng-ko po ang a-pel-yi-do ko)

▶ **How do you spell your family name?**
Ano po ang ispeling ng apelyido ninyo?
(A-no po ang is-pe-ling nang a-pel-yi-do nin-yo)

Name Card   *tarheta (tar-he-ta)*

▶ **Here is my name card.**
Heto po ang tarheta ko.
(He-to po ang tar-he-ta ko)

▶ **May I have your name card?**
Puwede ko po bang makuha ang tarheta ninyo?
(Pwe-de ko po bang ma-ku-ha ang tar-he-ta nin-yo)

▶ **Pleased to meet you.**
Ikinagagalak ko pong makilala kayo.
(I-ki-na-ga-ga-lak ko pong ma-ki-la-la ka-yó)

Age   *taong gulang* (ta-óng gu-lang);
             edad (e-dad)

► **How old are you?**
   Ilang taong gulang na po kayo?/
   Ano po ang edad ninyo?
   (I-láng ta-óng gu-lang na po ka-yo)/
   (A-no po ang e-dád nin-yo)

THE TIES THAT BIND... FAMILY

family	*pamilya* (pa-mil-ya)
mother	*nanay* (na-nay)
father	*tatay* (ta-tay)
daughter/son	*anak* (a-nák)
grandmother	*lola* (lo-la)
grandmother	*lolo* (lo-lo)
brother/sister	*kapatid* (ka-pa-tíd)
grandson/granddaughter	*apo* (a-pó)
wife/husband	*asawa* (a-sa-wa)

► **This is my wife/husband.**
   Ito po ang asawa ko.
   (I-to po ang a-sa-wa ko)

► **He/she is my son/daughter.**
   Siya po ang anak ko./Anak ko po siya.
   (Si-ya po ang a-nak ko/A-nak ko po si-ya)

Have	***may*** *(may)*
	mayroon *(may-ro-ón)*
	meron *(me-ron)*

For possession, we use the words **may** (pronounced with a long *i* sound, like the English word "my"), **mayroon** *(may-ro-on)* and **meron**. All three mean "have," and we use **may** and **mayroon** depending on sentence structure. **May** is followed by a noun while **mayroon** is followed by a pronoun or the word **ba** used for questions. The only difference between **mayroon** and **meron** is the spelling; when we speak, it is more natural to say "**meron**."

► **Do you have a son/daughter?**
May anak po ba kayo?/
Mayroon po ba kayong anak?/
Meron po ba kayong anak?
(May a-nák po ba ka-yo)/
(May-ro-on po ba ka-yong a-nák)/
(Me-ron po ba ka-yong a-nák)

► **I have a son/daughter.**
May anak po ako.
(May a-nák po a-ko)

► **I am not married./I don't have a husband/wife.**
Wala po akong asawa.
(Wa-la po a-kong a-sa-wa)

► **I don't have children.**
Wala po akong anak.
(Wa-la po a-kong a-nák)

► **Do you have grandchildren?**
May mga apo po ba kayo?
(May ma-nga a-pó po ba ka-yo)

► **I have grandchildren.**
May mga apo ako./
Mayroon akong mga apo./
Meron akong mga apo.
(May ma-nga a-pó a-ko)/
(May-ro-on a-kong ma-nga a-pó)/
(Me-ron a-kong ma-nga a-pó)

Ready   *handa (han-da)*

► **Are you ready?**
Handa ka na ba?
(Han-da ka na ba)

   Handa na po ba kayo? (formal)
   (Han-da na po ba ka-yo)

▶ **Yes. I'm ready.**
Oo. Handa na ako.
(O-o. Han-dâ na a-ko)

  Opo. Handa na po ako. (formal)
  (O-po. Han-dâ na po a-ko)

▶ **Not yet.**
Hindi pa po.
(Hin-dî pa po)

▶ **Come on!/Let's go!**
Halika na.
(Ha-li-ka na)

  Halina po kayo. (formal)
  (Ha-li-na po ka-yo)

A LITTLE RESPECT, PLEASE: PERSONAL TITLES

Although there are traditional personal titles in Filipino/Tagalog, in recent years, it is common to use titles in English. Note that when a title is said with a name, the linker **na**, contracted into "**ng**," is used.

Miss	*Binibini* (Bi-ni-bi-ni)
Miss Roque	*Binibining Roque*
	(Bi-ni-bi-ning Ro-ke)
Mr.	*Ginoo* (Gi-no-o)
Mr. Balmaceda	*Ginoong Balmaceda*
	(Gi-no-ong Bal-ma-ce-da)
Mrs.	*Ginang* (Gi-nang)
Mrs. Nemenzo	*Ginang Nemenzo*
	(Gi-nang Ne-men-zo)

ACADEMIC TITLES

Dean	*Dekano* (De-ka-no)
Professor	*Propesor* (Pro-pe-sór)
Associate Dean	*Katuwang na dekano*
	(Ka-tu-wang na de-ka-no)
Scholar	*Iskolar* (Is-ko-lar)
Teacher	*Guro* (Gu-ro)

► **This is Dean Tolentino.**
   Si Dekano Tolentino po ito.
   (Si De-ka-no To-len-ti-no po i-to)

► **Professor Raymundo is my teacher.**
   Guro ko po si Propesor Raymundo.
   (Gu-ro ko po si Pro-pe-sor Ray-mun-do)

BUSINESS AND PROFESSIONAL TITLES

As mentioned earlier, it is common in the Philippines to address people by their professional titles—for example, Engineer Gealogo, Attorney Abad, Architect Gonzales.

Ambassador	*embahador* (em-ba-ha-dor)
Architect	*arkitekto* (ar-ki-tek-to)
Artist	*artista* (ar-tis-ta)
Athlete	*atleta* (at-le-ta)
Businessman	*negosyante* (ne-gos-yan-te)
Dentist	*dentista* (den-tis-ta),
	addressed as "Doctor"...for example:

▶ **Dr. Larobis is my dentist.**
   Si Dr. Larobis po ang dentista ko.
   (Si Dok-tor La-ro-bis po ang den-tis-ta ko)

Doctor	*doktor/doktora*
	(dok-tór/dok-to-ra)
Engineer	*inhinyero* (in-hin-ye-ro)
Farmer	*magsasaka* (mag-sá-sa-ká)
Government official	*opisyal ng gobyerno*
	(o-pis-yál nang gob-yer-no)
Homemaker	*maybahay* (may-ba-hay)
Journalist	*mamamahayag*
	(ma-ma-má-ha-yág)

Lawyer	***abugado*** *(a-bu-ga-do)*
Nurse	***nars*** *(nars)*
Office worker	***kawani*** *(ka-wa-ní)*
Painter	***pintor*** *(pin-tór)*
Poet	***makata*** *(ma-ka-ta)*
Politician	***politiko*** *(po-li-ti-ko)*
Secretary	***sekretarya*** *(sek-re-tar-ya)*
Worker	***manggagawa*** *(mang-ga-ga-wa)*
Writer	***manunulat*** *(má-nu-nu-lát)*

WHO, WHAT, WHY...
ASKING FOR ANYTHING

Who?   *sino (si-no)*

▶ **Who are you?**
   Sino po silá?
   Here, in order to sound polite, the most formal way
   is used. Using the first person [**ka**] (singular) or
   [**kayo**] (plural) is not advised because one might
   sound rude.

▶ **Who is that?**
   Sino po iyon?
   (Si-no po i-yon)

► **Who is that man?**
Sino po ang lalaking iyon?
(Si-no po ang la-la-king i-yon)

► **Who is that woman?**
Sino po ang babaeng iyon?
(Si-no po ang ba-ba-eng i-yon)

What? *ano (a-nó)*

► **What is this?**
Ano po ito?
(A-no po i-to)

► **What is the price?**
Ano po ang presyo nito?
(A-no po ang pres-yo ni-to)

► **What did you say?**
Ano po ang sinabi ninyo?
(A-no po ang si-na-bi nin-yo)

► **What does ___ mean?**
Ano po ang ibig sabihin ng ___ ?
(A-no po ang i-big sa-bi-hin ng ___)

When?   *kailan (ka-i-lán)*

▶ **When will we start?**
   Kailan po tayo magsisimula?
   (Ka-i-lan po ta-yo mag-sí-si-mu-lá)

▶ **When is the meeting?**
   Kailan po ang miting?
   (Ka-i-lan po ang mi-ting)

▶ **When is the party?**
   Kailan po ang party?
   (Ka-i-lan po ang par-ty)

Where?   *nasaan (na-sa-an)*
                (used only for location)

▶ **Where is Luneta Park?**
   Nasaan ang Luneta Park?
   (Na-sa-an ang Lu-ne-ta Park)

▶ **Where is Quezon City?**
   Nasaan ang Quezon City?
   (Na-sa-an ang Ke-zon si-ti)

Where?   *saan (sa-án)* (used only with verbs)

► **Where do you live?**
  Saan ka nakatira?
  (Sa-an ka na-ka-ti-ra)

► **Where are you going?**
  Saan po kayo pupunta?
  (Sa-an po ka-yo pu-pun-ta)

Why?   *bakit (ba-kit)*

► **Why?**
  Bakit po?
  (Ba-kit po)

► **Why not?**
  Bakit po hindi?
  (Ba-kit po hin-di)

How?   *paano (pa-a-no)* (used with verbs)

► **How will you go to the hotel?**
  Paano kayo pupunta sa hotel?
  (Pa-a-no ka-yo pu-pun-ta sa ho-tel)

▶ **How will you pay?**
Paano kayo magbabayad?
(Pa-a-no ka-yo mag-ba-ba-yad)

▶ **How do you say…**
Paano mo sasabihin na…
(Pa-a-no mo sa-sa-bi-hin na)

How?   *gaano (ga-a-no)* (used for measuring)

How big?   *gaano kalaki (ga-a-no ka-la-kí)*

▶ **How big is the bag?**
Gaano po kalaki ang bag?
(Ga-a-no po ka-la-ki ang bag)

How long?   *gaano kahaba (ga-a-no ka-ha-ba)*

▶ **How long is the line?**
Gaano po kahaba ang linya?
(Ga-a-no po ka-ha-ba ang lin-ya)

How far?   *gaano kalayo* *(ga-a-no ka-la-yo)*

► **How far is the park?**
Gaano po kalayo ang parke?
(Ga-a-no po ka-layo ang par-ke)

How many? *ilan* *(i-lán)*

► **How many sandwiches?**
Ilan pong sandwich?
(I-lan pong sand-wich)

► **How many bags?**
Ilang pong bag?
(I-lan pong bag)

How much? *magkano* *(mag-ka-no)*

► **How much is the bag?**
Magkano po ang bag?
(Mag-ka-no po ang bag)

This   *ito (i-tó)*

▶ **What is this?**
Ano po ito?
(A-no po i-to)

That   *iyan (i-yán)*
                (sometimes pronounced as *'yan*)

▶ **What is that?**
Ano po iyan?
(A-no po i-yan)

That (over there)   *iyon (i-yón)*
                         (sometimes pronounced as *'yon*)

▶ **What is that (over there)?**
Ano po iyon?
(A-no po i-yon)

▶ **Who is that (over there)?**
Sino po iyon?
(Si-no po i-yón)

Which?   *alin* *(a-lín)*

▶ **Which would you like, tea or coffee?**
Alin ang gusto mo, kape o tsaa?
(A-lin ang gus-to mo, ka-pé o tsa-á)

   Alin po ang gusto ninyo, kape o tsaa? (formal)
(A-lin po ang gusto nin-yo, ka-pe o tsa-á)

▶ **Which bag is yours?**
Aling bag ang iyo?
(A-ling bag ang i-yo)

   Aling bag po ang inyo? (formal)
(A-ling bag po ang in-yo)

How old are you?
Ilang taong gulang na po kayo?

I'm twenty years old?
Dalawang taong gulang na po ako.

I have four brothers.
Mayroon po akong apat na kapatid na lalaki.

How many brothers do you have?
Ilan ang kapatid mong lalaki?

PART TWO
Numbers and Counting

There are two ways of counting in Filipino: the indigenous way in Tagalog, and the adapted Spanish way. We'll start with the indigenous way. You can find the adapted "Spanish" way on page 72, in "Telling Time." Both indigenous Tagalog and adapted Spanish ways are used for money and time, but many people prefer the adapted Spanish.

1, 2, 3: THE CARDINAL NUMBERS IN TAGALOG/FILIPINO

1	**Isa**	*(i-sá)*
2	**Dalawa**	*(da-la-wá)*
3	**Tatlo**	*(tat-ló)*
4	**Apat**	*(a-pat)*
5	**Lima**	*(li-má)*
6	**Anim**	*(a-nim)*
7	**Pito**	*(pi-tó)*
8	**Walo**	*(wa-ló)*
9	**Siyam**	*(si-yá)*
10	**Sampu**	*(sam-pû)*
11	**Labing-isa**	*(la-bíng-i-sá)*

12	**Labindalawa** *(la-bín-da-la-wá)*
13	**Labintatlo** *(la-bín-tat-ló)*
14	**Labing-apat** *(la-bing-a-pat)*
15	**Labinlima** *(la-bín-li-má)*
16	**Labing-anim** *(la-bing-a-nim)*
17	**Labimpito** *(la-bim-pi-tó)*
18	**Labingwalo** *(la-bing-wa-ló)*
19	**Labinsiyam** *(la-bin-si-yám)*
20	**Dalawampu** *(da-la-wam-pû)*
21	**Dalawampu't isa** *(da-la-wam-put i-sa)*
22	**Dalwampu't dalawa** *(da-la-wam-put da-la-wa)*
23	**Dalawampu't tatlo** *(da-la-wam-put tat-lo)*
24	**Dalawampu't apat** *(da-la-wam-put a-pat)*
25	**Dalawampu't lima** *(da-la-wam-put li-ma)*
26	**Dalawampu't anim** *(da-la-wam-put a-nim)*
27	**Dalawampu't pito** *(da-la-wam-put pi-to)*
28	**Dalawampu't walo** *(da-la-wam-put wa-lo)*
29	**Dalawampu't siyam** *(da-la-wam-put si-yam)*
30	**Tatlumpu** *(tat-lum-pû)*
40	**Apatnapu** *(á-pat-na-pû)*
50	**Limampu** *(li-mam-pû)*
60	**Animnapu** *(a-nim-na-pû)*
70	**Pitumpu** *(pi-tum-pû)*
80	**Walumpu** *(wa-lum-pû)*
90	**Siyamnapu** *(si-yam-na-pû)*
100	**Sandaan** *(san-da-an)*
200	**Dalawang daan** *(da-la-wang da-an)*
1000	**Sanlibo** *(san-li-bo)*

10,000	*Sampung libo* (sam-pung li-bo)
100,000	*Sandaang libo* (san-da-ang li-bo)
1,000,000	*Isang milyon* (i-sang mil-yon)
1,000,000,000	*Isang bilyon* (i-sang bil-yon)

COUNTING PEOPLE, OBJECTS, AND BUILDINGS

▶ **How many people are in the room?**
   Ilan po ang tao sa kuwarto?
   (I-lán po ang ta-o sa kwar-to)

NOTE: "**Kuwarto**" in most dictionaries is shown as *ku-war-to*. However, it is more common to hear it as *kwar-to*.

▶ **There are three people in the room.**
   May tatlong tao po sa kuwarto.
   (May tat-long ta-o po sa kwar-to)

▶ **How many sisters do you have?**
   Ilan ang kapatid mong babae?
   (I-lán ang ka-pa-tíd mong ba-ba-e)

   Ilan po ang kapatid ninyong babae? (formal)
   (I-lán po ang ka-pa-tíd nin-yong ba-ba-e)

► **I have two sisters.**
***Mayroon/Meron po akong dalawang kapatid
na babae.***
*(May-ro-ón/Me-ron po a-kóng da-la-wáng ka-pa-
tíd na ba-ba-e)*

► **How many brothers do you have?**
Ilan ang kapatid mong lalaki?
(I-lán ang ka-pa-tíd mong la-la-ki)

Ilan po ang kapatid ninyong babae? (formal)
(I-lán po ang ka-pa-tíd nin-yong ba-ba-e)

► **I have four brothers.**
***Mayroon/Meron po akong apat na kapatid na
lalaki.***
*(May-ro-on/Me-ron po a-kong a-pat na ka-pa-tíd
na la-la-ki)*

► **How many books do you have?**
Ilan ang libro mo?
(I-lán ang lib-ró mo)

Ilan po ang libro ninyo? (formal)
(I-lán po ang lib-ró nin-yo)

► **I have two books.**
Mayroon/Meron po akong dalawang libro.
(May-ro-on/Me-ron po a-kong da-la-wang lib-ró)

▶ **How many hotels are there in Manila?**
   Ilan po ang hotel sa Maynila?
   (I-lán po ang ho-tel sa May-ni-la)

▶ **There are twenty hotels in Manila.**
   Mayroon/Meron pong dalawampung hotel sa Maynila.
   (May-ro-on/Me-ron da-la-wam-pung ho-tel sa May-ni-la)

▶ **How many building are there on campus?**
   Ilan po ang building sa campus?
   (I-lan po ang bil-ding sa cam-pus)

▶ **There are ten buildings on campus.**
   Mayroon/Meron pong sampung building sa campus.
   (May-ro-on/Me-ron pong sam-púng bil-ding sa cam-pus)

COUNTING PAPER AND LIQUID

▶ **How many pieces of paper would you like?**
   Ilang piraso ng papel ang gusto ninyo?
   (I-láng pi-ra-so nang pa-pél ang gus-tó nin-yo)

▶ **I would like five pieces of paper.**
   Gusto ko po ng limang pirasong papel.
   (Gus-tó ko po nang li-mang pi-ra-song pa-pel)

▶ **How many bottles of water do you have?**
Ilan po ang bote ng tubig ninyo?
(I-lán po ang bo-te nang tu-big nin-yó)

▶ **How many cups of milk do you need?**
Ilan pong tasa ng gatas ang kailangan ninyo?
(I-lán pong ta-sa nang ga-tas ang ka-i-la-ngan nin-yó)

age   *taong gulang* (ta-óng gu-lang);
               edad (e-dád)

▶ **How old are you?**
Ilang taong gulang ka na?
(I-lang ta-ong gu-lang ka na)

Ilang taong gulang na po kayo? (formal)
(I-lang ta-ong gu-lang na po ka-yo)

▶ **I am twenty years old.**
Dalawampung taong gulang na po ako.
(Da-la-wam-pung ta-ong gu-lang na po a-kó)

▶ **How old is your mother?**
Ilang taon na ang nanay mo?
(I-lang ta-on na ang na-nay mo)

▶ **My mother is forty-five years old.**
Apatnapu't limang taong gulang na po ang nanay ko.

(A-pat-na-put li-mang ta-ong gu-lang na po ang na-nay ko)

1ST, 2ND, 3RD: THE ORDINAL NUMBERS

first	*Una* (u-na)
second	*Ikalawa* (i-ka-la-wá);
	Pangalawa (pa-nga-la-wá)
third	*Ikatlo* (i-kat-lo);
	Pangatlo (pa-ngat-ló)
fourth	*Ika-apat* (i-ka-a-pat);
	Pang-apat (pang-a-pat)
fifth	*Ikalima* (i-ka-li-ma);
	Panlima (pan-li-má)
sixth	*Ika-anim* (i-ka-a-nim);
	Pang-anim (pang-a-nim)
seventh	*Ikapito* (i-ka-pi-tó);
	Pampito (pam-pi-tó)
eighth	*Ika-walo* (i-ka-wa-ló);
	Pangwalo (pang-wa-ló)
ninth	*Ika-siyam* (i-ka-si-yám);
	Pangsiyam (pang-si-yám)
tenth	*Ika-sampu* (i-ka-sam-pû);
	Pangsampu (pang-sam-pû)

▶ **I am the second child in my family.**
Pangalawang anak ako sa pamilya.
(Pa-nga-la-wang a-nák a-ko sa pa-mil-ya)

▶ **The second car is my car.**
Kotse ko ang ikalawang kotse.
(Kot-se ko ang i-ka-la-wang kot-se)

▶ **I am third in my class.**
Pangatlo ako sa klase ko.
(Pa-ngat-lo a-ko sa kla-se ko)

▶ **The first seat is my seat.**
Silya ko ang unang upuan.
(Sil-ya ko ang u-nang u-pu-an)

TELLING TIME

time	*oras (o-ras)*	(in the sense of hours)
time	*panahon (pa-na-hón)*	(as in period of time)
second	*segundo (se-gun-do)*	
minute	*minuto (mi-nu-to)*	
hour	*oras (o-ras)*	
morning	*umaga (u-ma-ga)*	
afternoon	*hapon (ha-pon)*	
evening	*gabi (ga-bí)*	
A.M.	*ng umaga (nang u-ma-ga)*	

P.M.	***ng hapon*** *(nang ha-pon)* (in the afternoon)	
	ng gabi *(nang ga-bí)* (in the evening)	
dawn	***madaling-araw*** *(ma-da-ling-a-raw)*	
twilight	***dapithapon*** *(da-pit-ha-pon)*	
noon	***tanghali*** *(tang-ha-li)*	
midnight	***hatinggabi*** *(há-ting-ga-bí)*	

There are two ways of telling time in Tagalog/Filipino. One is through indigenous Tagalog words; the other is through words derived from Spanish.

Here are the two ways by which hours are expressed:

ENGLISH	SPANISH DERIVED	TAGALOG
1 o'clock	***ala-una*** *(a-la-u-na)*	***ika-isa*** *(i-ka-i-sá)*
2 o'clock	***alas-dos*** *(a-las-dos)*	***ika-dalawa*** *(i-ka-da-la-wá)*
3 o'clock	***alas-tres*** *(a-las-trés)*	***ika-tatlo*** *(i-ka-tat-ló)*
4 o'clock	***alas-kuwatro*** *(a-las-ku-wat-ro; also a-las-kwat-ro)*	***ika-apat*** *(i-ka-a-pat)*
5 o'clock	***alas-singko*** *(a-las-sing-ko)*	***ika-lima*** *(i-ka-li-má)*
6 o'clock	***alas-sais*** *(a-las-sa-ís)*	***ika-anim*** *(i-ka-a-nim)*

ENGLISH	SPANISH DERIVED	TAGALOG
7 o'clock	***alas-siyete***	***ika-pito***
	(a-las-si-ye-te;	*(i-ka-pi-tó)*
	also *a-las-ye-te)*	
8 o'clock	***alas-otso***	***ika-walo***
	(a-las-ot-so)	*(i-ka-wa-ló)*
9 o'clock	***alas-nuwebe***	***ika-siyam***
	(a-las-nu-we-be;	*(i-ka-si-yám)*
	also *a-las-nwe-be)*	
10 o'clock	***alas-diyes***	***ika-sampu***
	(a-las-diyes)	*(i-ka-sam-pû)*
11 o'clock	***alas-onse***	***ika-labing-isa***
	(a-las-on-se)	*(Ika-la-bíng-isá)*
12 o'clock	***alas-dose***	***ika-labindalawa***
	(a-las-do-se)	*(Ika-la-bín-da-la-wá)*

For minutes, you can use either the Spanish-derived words or the indigenous Tagalog words.

after	***makalipas*** *(ma-ka-li-pas)*
before	***bago*** *(ba-go)*
15	***kinse*** *(kin-se)*
30	***medya*** *(med-ya);* ***kalahati*** *(ka-la-ha-ti)*
	(Both of these words mean, literally, "half.")

Here are some examples:

► **It is 1:05.**
Ala-una singko na./
Limang minuto na makalipas ang ika-isa.
(A-la-u-na sing-ko na)/
(Li-mang mi-nu-to na ma-ka-li-pas ang i-ka-i-sa)

► **It is 3:15.**
Alas-tres kinse na./
Labinlimang minuto na makalipas ang ika-tatlo.
(A-las-tres kin-se na)/
(La-bin-li-mang mi-nu-to na ma-ka-li-pas ang
i-ka-tat-lo)

► **It is 4:30.**
Alas kuwatro y medya na./
Tatlumpung minuto na makalipas ang ika-apat.
(A-las-ku-wat-ro y med-ya na)/
(Tat-lum-púng mi-nu-to na ma-ka-li-pas ang
i-ka-a-pat)

___ of minutes before ___
menos __ para __ (literally, minus X before Y)
(me-nos ___ pa-ra ___)

▶ **It is 7:50.**
Menos diyes para alas-otso na./
Sampung minuto na bago ang ika-walo.
(Me-nos di-yes pa-ra a-las ot-so na)/
(Sam-pung mi-nu-to na ba-go ang i-ka-wa-lo)

▶ **It is 12:00 midnight.**
Alas-dose ng hatinggabi na./
Ika-labindalawa ng hatinggabi na.
(A-las-do-se ng ha-ting-ga-bi na)/
(I-ka-la-bin-da-la-wa nang ha-ting-ga-bi na)

▶ **It is 12:10 p.m.**
Alas-dose diyes ng tanghali na./
Sampung minuto na makalipas ang ika-la-
bindalawa ng tanghali.
(A-las do-se di-yes nang tang-ha-li na)/
(Sam-pung mi-nu-to na ma-ka-li-pas ang i-ka-la-
bin-da-la-wa nang tang-ha-li)

▶ **What time is it?**
Anong oras na?
(A-nong o-ras na)

Anong oras na po? (formal)
(A-nong o-ras na po)

► **It is 3:30 p.m.**
Alas-tres y medya na po ng hapon./
Ika-tatlo at kalahati na po ng hapon.
(A-las tres ee med-ya na po nang ha-pon)/
(I-ka-tat-lo at ka-la-ha-ti na po nang ha-pon)

► **It is 5:00 a.m.**
Alas-singko na po ng madaling-araw./
Ika-lima na po ng madaling-araw.
(A-las sing-ko na po nang ma-da-ling-a-raw)/
(I-ka-li-ma na po nang ma-da-ling-a-raw)

YESTERDAY, TODAY, TOMORROW

Yesterday	*kahapon (ka-ha-pon)*
Last night	*kagabi (ka-ga-bí)*
Today	*ngayong araw na ito*
	(nga-yong a-raw na i-to)
This morning	*ngayong umaga*
	(nga-yong u-ma-ga)
This afternoon	*ngayong hapon*
	(nga-yong ha-pon)
This evening	*ngayong gabi (nga-yong ga-bí)*
Tomorrow morning	*bukas nang umaga*
	(bú-kas nang u-ma-ga)
Tomorrow afternoon	*bukas nang hapon*
	(bú-kas nang ha-pon)

Tomorrow evening   *bukas nang gabi*
                         (bu-kas nang ga-bí)

▶ **When is the party?**
Kailan ang party?
(Ka-i-lan ang par-ti)

▶ **The party is tomorrow evening.**
Bukas nang gabi ang party.
(Bu-kas nang ga-bi ang par-ti)

▶ **When is the meeting?**
Kailan ang miting/pulong?
(Ka-i-lan ang mi-ting/pu-long)

▶ **The meeting is tomorrow morning.**
Bukas nang umaga ang miting/pulong.
(Bu-kas nang u-ma-ga ang mi-ting/pu-long)

▶ **Let's see each other tomorrow.**
Magkita tayo bukas.
(Mag-ki-ta ta-yo bu-kas)

DAYS OF THE WEEK

Monday   *Lunes (Lu-nes)*
Tuesday   *Martes (Mar-tés)*

Wednesday	***Miyerkoles*** *(Mi-yer-ko-les)*
Thursday	***Huwebes*** *(Hu-we-bes)*
Friday	***Biyernes*** *(Bi-yer-nes)*
Saturday	***Sabado*** *(Sá-ba-dó)*
Sunday	***Linggo*** *(Ling-gó)*
every day	***araw-araw*** *(a-raw-a-raw)*
every	***tuwing*** *(tu-wing)*

▶ **What day is today?**
Anong araw ngayon?
(A-nong a-raw nga-yon)

▶ **Today is Monday.**
Lunes ngayon.
(Lu-nes nga-yon)

▶ **When do you go to the university?**
Kailan ka pumupunta sa unibersidad?
(Ka-i-lan ka pu-mu-pun-ta sa u-ni-ber-si-dad)

▶ **I go to the university every day.**
Pumupunta ako sa unibersidad araw-araw.
(Pu-mu-pun-ta a-ko sa u-ni-ber-si-dad a-raw-a-raw)

▶ **When do you go to the gym?**
Kailan ka pumupunta sa gym?
(Ka-i-lan ka pu-mu-pun-ta sa gym)

▶ **I go to the gym on Tuesdays and Thursdays.**
Pumupunta ako sa gym tuwing Martes at Hu-
webes.
(Pu-mu-pun-ta a-ko sa gym tu-wing Mar-tes at Hu-
we-bes)

THIS WEEK, NEXT WEEK...

week	*linggo* (ling-gó)
every week	*linggo-linggo* (ling-gó-ling-gó)
this week	*ngayong linggo na ito*
	(nga-yong ling-gó na i-to)
last week	*noong nakaraang linggo*
	(no-ong na-ka-ra-ang ling-gó)
next week	*sa susunod na linggo*
	(sa su-su-nod na ling-gó)
week after next	*sa makalawang linggo*
	(sa ma-ka-la-wang ling-gó)
this weekend	*sa darating na Sabado't Linggo*
	(sa da-ra-ting na Sa-ba-do't Ling-gó)
calendar	*kalendaryo* (ka-len-dar-yo)

▶ **When is your flight?**
Kailan ang flight mo?
(Ka-i-lan ang flight mo)

▶ **My flight is next week.**
Sa susunod na linggo ang flight ko.
(Sa su-su-nod na ling-go ang flight ko)

▶ **How often do you watch a movie?**
Gaano kadalas ka nanonood ng sine?
(Ga-a-no ka-da-lás ka na-no-no-od nang si-ne)

▶ **I watch a movie every week.**
Nanonood ako ng sine linggo-linggo.
(Na-no-no-od a-ko nang si-ne ling-go-ling-go)

THE MONTHS

January	*Enero (E-ne-ro)*
February	*Pebrero (Peb-re-ro)*
March	*Marso (Mar-so)*
April	*Abril (Ab-ríl)*
May	*Mayo (Ma-yo)*
June	*Hunyo (Hun-yo)*
July	*Hulyo (Hul-yo)*
August	*Agosto (A-gos-to)*
September	*Setyembre (Set-yem-bre)*
October	*Oktubre (Ok-tub-re)*
November	*Nobyembre (Nob-yem-bre)*
December	*Disyembre (Dis-yem-bre)*

this month	***ngayong buwan na ito***
	(nga-yong bu-wan na i-to)
last month	***noong nakaraang buwan***
	(no-ong na-ka-ra-ang buwan)
next month	***sa susunod na buwan***
	(sa su-su-nod na bu-wan)
every month	***buwan-buwan*** *(bu-wan-bu-wan)*

► **When are you going to Japan?**
Kailan ka pupunta sa Japan?
(Ka-i-lan ka pu-pun-ta sa Ja-pan)

► **I will go to Japan in August.**
Pupunta ako sa Japan sa Agosto.
(Pu-pun-ta a-ko sa Ja-pan sa A-gos-to)

► **I will go to Canada next month.**
Pupunta ako sa Canada sa susunod na buwan.
(Pu-pun-ta a-ko sa Ca-na-da sa su-su-nod na bu-wan)

► **How often do you go to Cebu?**
Gaano kadalas ka pumupunta sa Cebu?
(Ga-a-no ka-da-lás ka pu-mu-pun-ta sa Se-bu)

► **I go to Cebu every month.**
Pumupunta ako sa Cebu buwan-buwan.
(Pu-mu-pun-ta a-ko sa Se-bu bu-wan-bu-wan)

THE YEAR

this year	***ngayong taon na ito***
	(nga-yong ta-ón na i-tó)
last year	***noong nakaraang taon***
	(no-óng na-ka-ra-ang ta-ón
next year	***sa susunod na taon***
	(sa su-su-nod na ta-ón)
every year	***taon-taon*** *(ta-ón-ta-ón)*
New Year's Day	***Bagong Taon*** *(Ba-gong Ta-ón)*

► **When did you go to Africa?**
Kailan ka pumunta sa Africa?
(Ka-i-lan ka pu-mun-ta sa Af-ri-ka)

► **I went to Africa last year.**
Pumunta ako sa Africa nitong nakaraang taon.
(Pu-mun-ta a-ko sa Af-ri-ka ni-tong na-ka-ra-ang ta-on)

► **I will graduate next year.**
Magtatapos ako sa susunod na taon.
(Mag-tá-ta-pós a-ko sa su-su-nod na ta-on)

► **How often do you take a vacation?**
Gaano kadalas ka nagbabakasyon?
(Ga-a-no ka-da-las ka nag-ba-ba-kas-yon)

► **I take a vacation every year.**
Nagbabakasyon ako taon-taon.
(Nag-ba-ba-kas-yon a-ko ta-on-ta-on)

► **When will you work for Philippine Publishing Company?**
Kailan ka magtatrabaho sa Philippine Publishing Company?
(Ka-i-lan ka mag-ta-tra-ba-ho sa Philippine Publishing Company)

► **This year.**
Ngayong taon na ito.
(Nga-yong ta-ón na i-tó)

PART THREE
Let's see/eat/do every-thing!

TRAVEL VOCABULARY AND USEFUL EXPRESSIONS

Many words used for transportation are derived from either English or Spanish. In some cases, the spelling has been adapted. Usually, it is fine to use either the English word or the Tagalog coined word, and/or to use the English spelling.

AIRPORT/AIRLINES

airport	*airport/paliparan* (pa-li-pa-ran)
airlines	*airlines*
fly	*lipad* (li-pád)
flight number	*flight number*

▶ I am going to Ninoy Aquino International Airport.
Pupunta po ako sa Ninoy Aquino International Airport.
(Pu-pun-ta po a-ko sa Ni-noy A-ki-no International Airport)

▶ **What is your airline?**
Ano po ang airlines ninyo?
(A-no po ang airlines nin-yo)

▶ **I want a Philippine Airlines flight.**
Gusto ko po ng flight na Philippine Airlines.
(Gus-to ko po nang flight na Philippine Airlines)

▶ **What time are you flying?**
Anong oras po ang lipad ninyo?
(A-nong o-ras po ang li-pad nin-yo)

▶ **I fly at 1:00 p.m.**
Ala-una ng hapon ang lipad ko.
(A-la-u-na nang ha-pon ang li-pád ko)

MONEY

Philippine currency is called **piso** and **peso**. Use **peso/s** when counting using Spanish derived words and use **piso** (never with the plural "s") when counting using indigenous Tagalog words.

ENGLISH	SPANISH DERIVED	TAGALOG
peso/s	*peso/s* (pe-so/s)	*piso* (pi-so)
cent/s	*sentimo/s*	*sentimo*
	(sen-ti-mó/s)	(sén-ti-mó)

Current coins are:

ENGLISH	SPANISH DERIVED	TAGALOG
One cent	***isang sentimo***	***isang sentimo***
	(i-sang sen-ti-mo)	*(i-sang sen-ti-mo)*
Five cents	***singko sentimos***	***limang sentimo***
	(sing-ko sen-ti-mos)	*(li-mang sen-ti-mo)*
Ten cents	***diyes sentimos***	***sampung sentimo***
	(di-yes sen-ti-mos)	*(sam-pung sen-ti-mo)*
Twenty-five cents	***beinte-singko sentimos***	***dalawampu't limang sentimo***
	(béyn-te-sing-ko sen-ti-mos)	*(da-law-wam-put li-mang sen-ti-mo)*
One peso	***peso*** *(pe-so)*	***piso*** *(pi-so)*
Five pesos	***singko pesos***	***limang piso***
	(sing-ko pe-sos)	*(li-mang pi-so)*
Ten pesos	***diyes pesos***	***sampung piso***
	(di-yes pe-sos)	*(sam-pung pi-so)*

Bank notes for 5 and 10 pesos are no longer printed but they can still be accepted. Current bank notes are:

ENGLISH	SPANISH DERIVED	TAGALOG
Twenty pesos	***beinte pesos***	***dalawampung piso***
	(beyn-te pe-sos)	*(da-la-wam-pung pi-so)*

Fifty pesos	*singkuwenta pesos* (sing-ku-wen-ta pe-sos)	*limampung piso* (li-mam-pung pi-so)
One hundred pesos	*siyento pesos* (si-yen-to pe-sos)	*sandaang piso* (san-da-ang pi-so)
Two hundred pesos	*dos siyentos* (dos si-yen-tos pe-sos)	*dalawandaang piso* (da-la-wang da-ang pi-so)
Five hundred pesos	*kinyentos* (kin-yen-tos)	*limandaang piso* (li-man-da-ang pi-so)
One thousand pesos	*mil* (mil)	*sanlibong piso* (san-li-bong pi-so)

(Note: *Mil* is used with a number to say two thousand (*dos mil*), three thousand (*tres mil*), etc. But you would not specify "*uno mil*."

Many words related to money and the exchanging of currency are derived from English. In some cases, the English is retained.

money	*pera* (pe-ra)
money changer	*money changer*; *nagpapalit ng pera* (nag-pa-pa-lit nang pe-ra)
exchange rate	*palitan* (pa-lí-tan)

U.S. dollars	**dolyar** *(dol-yár)*
Japanese yen	**yen** *(yen)*
check	**tseke** *(tse-ke)*
travelers' check	**travelers' check**
small change	**barya** *(bar-yá)*

► What is the current exchange?
   Ano po ang palitan ngayon?
   (A-no po ang pa-lí-tan nga-yón)

► The dollar exchange rate is 46 to 1.
   46 po ang palitan ng dolyar.
   (Ku-wa-ren-ta y sals po ang pa-li-tan nang dol-yar)

► Where can I change money?
   Saan po ako puwedeng magpapalit ng pera?
   (Sa-an po ako pu-we-deng mag-pa-pa-lit nang pe-ra)

► Do you change Japanese yen?
   Nagpapalit po ba kayo ng yen?
   (Nag-pa-pa-lit po ba ka-yo nang yen)

► I have no money.
   Wala po akong pera.
   (Wa-la po a-kong pe-ra)

► I have no money with me.
   Wala po akong dalang pera.
   (Wa-la po a-kong da-lang pe-ra)

▶ **I have no small change.**
  Wala po akong barya.
  (Wa-la po a-kong bar-ya)

▶ **Do you accept travelers' checks?**
  Tumatanggap po ba kayo ng travelers' check?
  (Tu-ma-tang-gap po ba ka-yo nang travelers' check)

▶ **Just small change please.**
  Barya lang po.
  (Bar-ya lang po)

TAXIS/FX OR GT EXPRESS SERVICE

Usually, one can simply hail taxis in the streets of Manila and in other major cities. Larger taxis are usually either the AUVs (Asian utility vehicles) or vans which can seat around eight people. Taxis which have special routes are the airport cabs and the Garage-Terminal Express taxis (popularly called the FX, short for the brand name Toyota FX), where passengers share the taxi from the "terminal" to a single destination.

taxi	***taksi*** *(tak-si)*
driver	***tsuper*** *(tsu-pér)*; ***drayber*** *(dray-ber)*
passenger	***pasahero*** *(pa-sa-he-ro)*

payment	***bayad*** *(ba-yad)*
change	***sukli*** *(suk-lí)*

▶ **Where can I get a taxi?**
Saan po ako puwedeng kumuha ng taksi?
(Sa-an po a-ko pu-we-deng ku-mu-ha nang tak-si)

▶ **Can you call a taxi for me?**
Puwede po ba kayong tumawag ng taksi para sa akin?
(Pu-we-de po ba ka-yong tu-ma-wag nang tak-si pa-ra sa a-kin)

▶ **Please take me to the airport.**
Pakihatid po ako sa airport.
(Pa-ki-ha-tid po a-ko sa airport)

▶ **Please take me to this address.**
Pakihatid po ako sa address na ito.
(Pa-ki-ha-tid po a-ko sa ad-res na i-to)

▶ **Please take me to ___ Hotel.**
Pakihatid po ako sa __ Hotel.
(Pa-ki-ha-tid po a-ko sa __ Hotel)

▶ **How much does it cost to go to the airport by taxi?**
Magkano po ang papunta sa airport kung magta-taksi?
(Mag-ka-no po ang pa-pun-ta sa air-port kung mag-ta-tak-si)

▶ **How much does it cost from ___ to ___?**
Magkano ho mula __ hanggang __?
(Mag-ka-no ho mu-la __ hang-gang __)

▶ **Please wait for me.**
Pakihintay po ako.
(Pa-ki-hin-tay po a-ko)

▶ **How much?**
Magkano po?
(Mag-ka-no po)

▶ **Here is my payment.**
Heto po ang bayad ko.
(He-to po ang ba-yad ko)

DIRECTIONS

▶ **Go straight.**
Dumiretso po kayo.
(Du-mi-ret-so po ka-yo)

left   *kaliwa (ka-li-wâ)*

▶ **Turn left.**
  Kaliwa po.
  (Ka-li-wa po)

▶ **Please turn left at the next corner.**
  Kumaliwa po kayo sa susunod na kanto.
  (Ku-ma-li-wa po ka-yo sa su-su-nod na kan-to)

right   *kanan (ka-nan)*

▶ **Turn right.**
  Kanan po.
  (Ka-nan po)

▶ **Please turn right at the next corner.**
  Kumanan po kayo sa susunod na kanto.
  (Ku-ma-nan po ka-yo sa su-su-nod na kan-to)

here   *dito (di-to)/rito (ri-to)*

▶ **Please stop here.**
  Dito na po. (literally, Here already.)
  Pakihinto po rito. (literally, Please stop here.)
  (Di-to na po/Pa-ki-hin-to po ri-to)

▶ **Please wait here.**
   Pakihintay po ako rito.
   (Pa-ki-hin-tay po a-ko ri-to)

▶ **Please let me off here.**
   Pakibaba po ako rito.
   (Pa-kí-ba-ba po a-ko ri-to)

there	*diyan (di-yan)/**riyan** (ri-yan)*
over there	*doon (do-on)/**roon** (ro-on)*

▶ **Please put my bag there.**
   Pakilagay po ang bag ko riyan.
   (Pa-ki-la-gay po ang bag ko ri-yan)

hurry	*nagmamadali (nag-ma-ma-da-li)*

▶ **I am in a hurry.**
   Nagmamadali po ako.
   (Nag-ma-ma-da-li po a-ko)

METRO MANILA TRAINS

There are three railway lines in Metro Manila as of 2011: the Philippine National Railways (PNR), which operates the Northrail and the Southrail (from Manila to neighboring provinces); the Line Rail Transit System (LRT), operating the yellow and purple lines; and the Metro Rail Transit (MRT), operating the blue line.

train	***tren** (tren)*; also called MRT and LRT
train station	***estasyon ng tren** (es-tas-yón nang tren)*

► **Do you have a train map in English?**
Mayroon po ba kayong mapa ng tren na nasa wikang Ingles?
(May-ro-on po ba ka-yong ma-pa ng tren na na-sa wi-kang Ing-gles)

► **Where is the train station?**
Nasaan po ang estasyon ng tren?
(Na-sa-an po ang es-tas-yon ng tren)

► **Where is the nearest train station?**
Nasaan po ang pinakamalapit na estasyon ng tren?
(Na-sa-an po ang pi-na-ka-ma-la-pit na es-tas-yon ng tren)

► **Where do I get off to go to go to ___?**
Saan po ako bababa para pumunta sa__?
(Sa-an po a-ko ba-ba-ba pa-ra pu-mun-ta sa ___)

ticket   *tiket (ti-ket)*

► **Where can I buy a ticket?**
Saan po ako puwedeng bumili ng tiket?
(Sa-an po a-ko pu-we-deng bu-mi-li nang ti-ket)

BUSES AND JEEPNEYS

Buses in the Philippines usually have conductors who collect fares and issue tickets. Jeepneys do not; the passenger can just pay the driver at any time while traveling. If the passenger is seated at the rear end of the jeepney and farther away from the driver, he/she asks fellow passengers to help him/her give the fare by passing it along to the front. There are no set schedules for intercity buses and jeepneys. Only buses that go to the provinces have set schedules.

bus	*bus (bas)*
bus that goes to the provinces or countryside	*pamprobinsiyang bus* *(pam-pro-bin-si-yang bas)*
bus station	*estasyon ng bus (es-tas-yon ng bas); paradahan ng bus* *(pá-ra-da-hán nang bas)* (literally, bus parking)

bus stop	*sakayan ng bus* (sa-ka-yan nang bas); *bus stop* (bas is-stap)
jeepney	*dyipni* (dyip-ni) (unique local vehicle originally made from army jeeps; seats 14–16 people)
jeepney stop	*sakayan ng dyipni* (sa-ka-yan ng dyip-ni); *jeepney stop* (dyip-ni is-stap)
fare	*pamasahe* (pa-ma-sa-he)

► **Is there a bus stop near here?**
May bus stop po bang malapit dito?/
May sakayan po ba ng bus na malapit dito?
(May bas is-stop po bang ma-la-pit di-to)/
(May sa-ka-yan po ba ng bas na ma-la-pit di-to)

► **Is there a bus station near here?**
May estasyon po ba ng bas na malapit dito?
(May es-tas-yon po ba nang bas na ma-la-pit di-to)

► **Where is the jeepney stop (here)?**
Saan po dito ang sakayan ng dyip?
(Sa-an po di-to ang sa-ka-yan nang dyip)

► **Which bus goes to Makati?**
Aling bus po ang pumupunta ng Makati?
(A-ling bas po ang pu-mu-pun-ta nang Ma-ka-ti)

▶ **Which jeepney goes to Fort Santiago?**
Aling dyipni po ang pumupunta sa Fort Santiago?
(A-ling dyip-ni po ang pu-mu-pun-ta sa Fort San-ti-a-go)

▶ **Which ___ goes to ___?**
Aling __ po ang pumupunta sa __?
(A-ling __ po ang pu-mu-pun-ta sa __)

▶ **Will this jeepney pass by the Manila post office?**
Dadaan po ba ang dyipni na ito sa Manila post office?
(Da-da-an po ba ang dyip-ni na ito sa Manila post office)

▶ **Here is my fare.**
Heto po ang bayad ko.
(He-to po ang ba-yad ko)

▶ **Please give my fare to the driver.**
Paabot po sa drayber ng bayad ko.
(Pa-a-bot po sa dray-ber nang ba-yad ko)

▶ **Please stop here!**
Para po!
(Para po)

▶ **Please let me off at the next jeepney stop.**
  Pakibaba po ako sa susunod na jeepney stop.
  (Pa-ki-ba-ba po a-ko sa su-su-nod na dyip-ni is-stap)

▶ **How much to go to Cubao?**
  Magkano ho hanggang Cubao?
  (Mag-ka-no ho hang-ggáng Cubao)

▶ **Where did you board (come from)?**
  Saan ho kayo galing?
  (Sa-an ho ka-yo ga-ling)

TRICYCLES

Tricycles, or more accurately, "motorized tricycles," also called "pedicab," are popular in the sidestreets of Metro Manila and in the countryside. They come in a variety of styles and colorful decorations, but usually for each, there is a sidecar or a a bicycle. A sidecar that can accommodate around 3-4 passengers. The tricycles are usually found near bus, train or jeepney stops, public market parking lots, and entrances to villages or residential districts.

The tricycle leaves its waiting place only when it is full. Sometimes, the driver will also ask you if you would rather not wait for other passengers and would just like to rent the tricycle for yourself.

Passengers are usually asked by the driver the street
where they want to be taken. When you get to your
street, give the tricycle driver the number of the house/
building.

wait	*maghintay (mag-hin-tay)*
other	*iba pa (i-ba pa)*
rent	*arkila (ar-ki-lá)*
to rent	*arkilahin (ar-ki-la-hin)*
passenger	*pasahero (pa-sa-he-ro)*
Mr. Driver	*mamang drayber (ma-mang dray-ber)*; used to address the driver
stop	*itabi (i-ta-bí)* (literal meaning: to park by the side of the road to enable the passenger to get off)

▶ **Would you like to wait for other passengers?**
*Gusto niyo pa bang maghintay ng iba pang
pasahero?*
*(Gus-to nyo pa bang mag-hin-tay nang iba pang
pa-sa-he-ro)*

▶ **Okay.**
Sige ho.
(Si-ge ho)

▶ **I will just rent this.**
Arkilahin ko na lang ho.
(Ar-ki-la-hin ko na lang ho)

▶ **Where are you going?**
Saan ho kayo?
(Sa-an ho ka-yo)

▶ **I am going to Adarna Street.**
Sa Adarna Street ho ako.
(Sa A-dar-na street ho a-ko)

▶ **Please let me off (there) at number 74.**
Diyan lang ho ako sa number 74.
(Jan lang ho a-ko sa number 74)

▶ **I am going to the market.**
Sa palengke ho ako.
(Sa pa-leng-ke ho a-ko)

▶ **Please stop at the blue house.**
Itabi niyo lang ho sa bahay na kulay blue.
(I-ta-bí nyo lang ho sa ba-hay na ku-lay blue)

▶ **How much is the fare?**
Magkano ho ang pamasahe?
(Mag-ka-no ho ang pa-ma-sa-he)

RENTAL CARS

car	**kotse** *(ko-tse)*
rental car	**pinaaarkilahang kotse** *(pi-na-a-ar-ki-la-hang ko-tse)*
driver	**tsuper** *(tsu-per)*; **drayber** *(dray-ber)*
driver's license	**lisensiya** *(li-sén-si-yá)*
parking lot	**paradahan** *(pá-ra-da-hán)*
gas station/ service station	**gasolinahan** *(gá-so-li-na-hán)*
mechanic's shop	**talyer** *(tal-yér)*
speed limit	**speed** limit

► I would like to rent a car.
  Gusto ko pong mag-arkila ng kotse.
  (Gus-to ko pong mag-ar-ki-la nang kot-se)

► Where can I rent a car?
  Saan po ako puwedeng mag-arkila ng kotse?
  (Sa-an po a-ko pu-we-deng mag-ar-ki-la nang kot-se)

► I also want a driver.
  Gusto ko rin po ng tsuper.
  (Gus-to ko rin po nang tsu-per)

▶ **How much by the day?**
   Magkano po ang isang araw?
   (Mag-ka-no po ang i-sang a-raw)

PHILIPPINE NATIONAL RAILWAYS ROUTES

The "rehabilitation" plan of Philippine National Railways recently resulted in new trains for the Manila-Bicol route. The so-called "Bicol Express" resumed the Manila-Quezon-Bicol route in 2011 on the 400-kilometer railroad. There are several classes of coaches: an air-conditioned "tourist class" with reclining seats at ₱548 per passenger; "sleeper coaches" from ₱700-800; and family suites which can accommodate four to six people per compartment at ₱950/berth; and the executive section with individualized compartments at ₱1,300. The estimated travel time is ten hours. There are also plans to revive northbound routes to Tuguegarao City in Cagayan and Laoag City in Ilocos Norte. Note that the coach names are in English—equivalents and not exact translations are provided below, but it is fine to say the terms in English.

train	***tren*** *(tren)*
express train	***ekspres na tren*** *(eks-pres na tren)*

local stops	***mga tinitigilang estasyon*** *(ma-nga ti-ni-ti-gi-lang es-tas-yon)/* ***mga hinihintuang estasyon*** *(ma-nga hi-ni-hin-tu-ang es-tas-yon)*
conductor	***konduktor*** *(kon-duktor)*
one-way ticket	***tiket na pang-isang sakay*** *(ti-ket na pang-i-sang sa-kay)*
round-trip ticket	***balikang tiket*** *(ba-li-kang ti-ket)*

▶ **Is there a dining car in this train?**
May restawran po ba sa tren na ito? (Literally, Is there a restaurant in this train?)
(May res-taw-ran po ba sa tren na i-to)

▶ **Where is the dining car in this train?**
Saan po ba ang restawran sa tren na ito?
(Sa-an po ba ang res-taw-ran sa tren na i-to)

▶ **Is there somewhere we can buy food in this train?**
May mabibilhan po ba ng pagkain sa tren na ito?
(May ma-bi-bil-han po ba nang pag-ka-in sa tren na i-to)

regular coaches	***tourist class; regular*** *(re-gu-lar)*
reclining seats	***mga upuang nagagalaw*** *(ma-nga u-pu-ang na-ga-ga-law)*

sleeper coaches	***may mga tulugan***
	(may ma-nga tu-lu-gán)
family suites	***pampamilya*** *(pam-pa-mil-ya)*
executive section	***pang-eksekyutib***
	(pang-ek-se-kyu-tib);
	pinaka-espesyal
	(pi-na-ka-es-pesy-yal)
	(literally, most special)

▶ **Is there air conditioning in this coach?**
May aircon po ba ang coach na ito?
(May air-con po ba ang coach na i-to)

▶ **I want a ticket in the sleeper coach.**
Gusto ko po ng tiket para sa coach na may mga tulugan.
(Gus-to ko po nang ti-ket pa-ra sa coach na may ma-nga tu-lu-gan)

▶ **How much is a ticket in the executive section?**
Magkano po ang tiket sa eksekyutib?
(Mag-ka-no po ang ti-ket sa ek-sek-yu-tib)

▶ **How many people can fit in the family suite?**
Ilan pong tao ang kasya sa suite na pampamilya?
(I-lan pong ta-o ang kas-ya sa swit na pam-pa-mil-ya)

► **Is the price of ₱950 for the whole suite or per person?**
   Ang presyong ₱950 po ba ay para sa buong suite o para sa bawat tao?
   (Ang pres-yong ₱950 po ba ay pa-ra sa bu-ong swit o pa-ra sa ba-wat ta-o)

► **What station is this?**
   Anong estasyon na po ba ito?
   (A-nong es-tas-yon na po ba i-to)

► **What is the next station?**
   Ano po ang susunod na estasyon?
   (A-no po ang su-su-nod na es-tas-yon)

► **I want to get off at Lucena.**
   Gusto ko pong bumaba sa Lucena.
   (Gus-to ko pong bu-ma-bá sa Lu-se-na)

HOTELS AND RESORTS

Metro Manila has a wide selection of hotels, from the very luxurious with ocean views to budget inns. Also, aside from major U.S. and European hotel chains, there are several "suite hotels" or "apartment hotels" offering extended stay discounts. Family-run bed and breakfasts are not common in Metro Manila. In the regions, especially on islands such as Boracay and Palawan, one can also find a variety of accommodations.

Please be careful of the word "motel" when asking about accommodations. In the Philippines, the word "motel" refers to establishments that offer brief room rentals (from three hours to overnight), catering to couples seeking privacy.

Although equivalents are provided below for room types, the English terms are usually used.

hotel	***hotel*** *(ho-tel)*
reservations	***reserbasyon*** *(re-sér-bas-yón)*
to confirm	***kumpirma*** *(kum-pir-ma)*
room	***kuwarto*** *(ku-war-to)*
room charge	***bayad sa kuwarto*** *(ba-yad sa ku-war-to)*
room key	***susi ng kuwarto*** *(su-si nang ku-war-to)*
single bed	***kamang pang-isahan***
	(ka-mang pang-i-sa-han)
double bed	***kamang pandalawahan***
	(ka-mang pan-da-la-wa-han)
bathroom	***banyo*** *(ban-yo)*
front desk	***front desk***
maid	***tagalinis ng kuwarto***
	(ta-ga-li-nis ng ku-war-to)

In Philippine culture, domestic workers are also called "maids" or in Tagalog/Filipino, **kasambahay** *(ka-sam-ba-hay)* (literally, someone in the same house) or **katulong** *(ka-tu-long)* (literally, helper).

hotel car service   serbis *(ser-bis)*
Refers to transportation sometimes provided by a hotel or resort to the airport, especially in more remote areas.

▶ **Can I pay with a credit card?**
   ***Puwede po ba akong magbayad sa pamamagi-
   tan ng credit card?/Puwede po ba akong magbayad gamit ang credit card?***
   *(Pu-we-de po ba a-kong mag-ba-yad sa pa-ma-ma-
   gi-tan nang credit card)/(Pu-we-de po ba a-kong
   mag-ba-yad ga-mit ang credit card)*

▶ **Do you take travelers' checks?**
   Tumatanggap po ba kayo ng travelers' checks?
   (Tu-ma-tang-gap po ba ka-yo nang travelers' checks)

▶ **Can I change my room?**
   Puwede po ba akong magpalit ng kuwarto?
   (Pu-we-de po ba akong mag-pa-lít nang ku-war-to)

▶ **There is a problem with my room.**
   May problema po sa kuwarto ko.
   (May prob-le-ma po sa ku-war-to ko)

TOILETS/RESTROOMS

bathroom	***banyo*** *(ban-yo)/* ***kubeta*** *(ku-be-ta)/* ***C.R.*** *(si-ar)*
toilet paper	***toilet paper***

Banyo is the general term that refers to both the bathing and toilet areas of a bathroom. **Kubeta** is a more specific term for toilets, but is a bit unpleasant to hear. Another popular term used is **c.r.**, which is short for "comfort room."

▶ **Where is the toilet?**
   Nasaan po ang banyo?/Nasaan po ang C.R.?
   (Na-sa-an po ang ban-yo?/Na-sa-an po ang si-ar)

SEASONS AND WEATHER

There are only two seasons in the Philippines: the dry/hot season from March to May, also known as the summer season, and the rainy season from June to November. The cooler months are December, January and February, and some people call this period the "cold season." Temperatures and humidity are relatively high especially during the summer months. Tropical storms and typhoons usually occur from July to October, sometimes causing floods.

dry/hot season/ summer	***tag-araw*** *(tág-a-ráw)*
rainy season	***tag-ulan*** *(tág-u-lán)*
cold season	***taglamig*** *(tág-la-míg)*
weather	***panahon*** *(pa-na-hón)*
	(note that **panahon** also means "time")
climate	***klima*** *(kli-ma)*
clouds	***ulap*** *(u-lap)*
rain	***ulan*** *(u-lán)*
hot/warm	***mainit*** *(ma-i-nit)*
cold	***malamig*** *(ma-la-míg)*
rainy	***maulan*** *(ma-u-lán)*
windy	***mahangin*** *(ma-ha-ngin)*
humid	***maalinsangan*** *(ma-a-lin-sa-ngan)*
storm/typhoon	***bagyo*** *(bag-yó)*
flood	***baha*** *(ba-hâ)*

► **How is the weather today?**
   Kumusta po ang panahon ngayon?
   (Ku-mus-ta po ang pa-na-hon nga-yon)

► **It looks like rain, doesn't it?**
   Mukhang uulan, hindi po ba?
   (Mu-kang u-u-lan, hin-di po ba)

► **It's awfully hot, isn't it?**
   Napakainit, hindi po ba?
   (Na-pa-ka-i-nit, hin-di po ba)

- ▶ **It's too hot.**
  Masyadong mainit.
  (Mas-ya-dong ma-i-nit)

- ▶ **It's raining!**
  Umuulan!
  (U-mu-u-lan)

- ▶ **Do you think it will rain tomorrow?**
  Uulan po kaya bukas?
  (U-u-lan po ka-ya bu-kas)

- ▶ **Do you think (the streets) will be flooded?**
  Babaha po kaya?
  (Ba-ba-ha po ka-ya)

- ▶ **Is there a typhoon/storm?**
  May bagyo po ba?
  (May bag-yo po ba)

- ▶ **What is tomorrow's weather forecast?**
  Ano po ang lagay ng panahon bukas?
  (A-no po ang la-gay nang pa-na-hon bu-kas)

TROPICAL STORMS

The Philippines is situated in a vast expanse of warm ocean water in the western rim of the Pacific Ocean, making it one of the most vulnerable countries to tropical storms. An average of eight or nine storms makes landfall in the Philippines in a year, resulting in floods, destruction of infrastructure, and crop devastation.

The Philippine Atmospheric, Geophysical, and Astronomical Services Administration (PAGASA) releases warnings through Public Storm Warning Signals, usually broadcast over television and radio. Pre-school classes are suspended at signal 1, elementary and high schools at signal 2, and colleges and universities at signals 3 and 4. The following table summarizes the estimated severity of the storms denoted by the signal's numbering and other pertinent details:

SIGNAL	WIND SPEEDS	OTHER PERTINENT DETAILS
#1	30 km/h to 60 km/h (19 mph–37 mph)	Expected within the next 36 hours; people are advised to listen to the latest weather bulletin
#2	60 km/h to 100 km/h (37 mph–62 mph)	Expected within the next 24 hours; people traveling by sea and air are cautioned to avoid unnecessary traveling

SIGNAL	WIND SPEEDS	OTHER PERTINENT DETAILS
#3	100 km/h to 185 km/h (62 mph–115 mph)	Expected within the next 18 hours; travel is risky; people are advised to seek shelter in strong buildings and evacuate from low-lying areas
#4	Over 185 km/h (115 mph)	Expected within 12 hours; potentially very destructive; people are advised to cancel all travel and outdoor activities; evacuation to safer shelters should have been completed

strong rain	*malakas na ulan*	*(ma-la-kás na u-lán)*
warning	*babala*	*(ba-ba-lâ)*
evacuate	*lumikas*	*(lu-mi-kas)*
safer place	*mas ligtas na lugar*	*(mas lig-tás na lu-gár)*

▶ **What is the storm signal now?**
   Ano na hong signal ng bagyo ngayon?
   (A-nó na hong signal nang bag-yó nga-yón)

► **Are all flights canceled?**
Kanselado na ba ang flights?
(Kan-se-la-do na ba ang flights)

► **Where (what streets) can we pass that are not flooded?**
Saan tayo puwedeng dumaan na walang baha?
(Sa-án ta-yo pwe-deng du-ma-an na wa-láng ba-hâ)

► **Do we need to evacuate?**
Kailangan ba nating lumikas?
(Ka-i-la-ngan ba na-ting lu-mi-kas)

► **It is signal no. 3.**
Signal no. 3 na.
(Sig-nal num-ber 3 na)

► **Do not go out of the house.**
Huwag kayong lumabas ng bahay.
('Wag ka-yóng lu-ma-bas ng ba-hay)

► **Let us evacuate.**
Lumikas na tayo.
(Lu-mi-kas na ta-yo)

► **Let us move to a safer place.**
Pumunta tayo sa mas ligtas na lugar.
(Pu-mun-tá ta-yo sa mas lig-tás na lu-gár)

EATING

Most menus in the Philippines are in English, and Filipino food with names in Tagalog/Filipino usually have descriptions in English.

breakfast	***almusal*** *(al-mu-sal)*
lunch	***tanghalian*** *(tang-ha-li-an)*
dinner	***hapunan*** *(ha-pu-nan)*
snack	***meryenda*** *(mer-yen-da)*/***minindal*** *(mi-nin-dâl)*
menu	***menu*** *(me-nú)*

▶ **Can I ask for a menu?**
   Puwede po bang makahingi ng menu?
   (Pu-we-de po bang ma-ka-hi-ngi nang me-nu)

▶ **I'm ready to order.**
   Handa na po akong mag-order.
   (Han-da na po a-kong mag-or-der)

▶ **I'm not yet ready to order.**
   Hindi pa po ako handang mag-order.
   (Hin-di pa po ako han-dang mag-or-der)

waiter	***weyter*** *(wey-ter)*
waitress	***waitress*** *(weyt-res)*
Filipino food	***pagkaing Filipino*** *(pag-ka-ing Fi-li-pi-no)*

Chinese food	***pagkaing Intsik*** *(pag-ka-ing Int-sik)*
dish	***putahe*** *(pu-ta-he)*
delicious	***masarap*** *(ma-sa-ráp)*
salty	***maalat*** *(ma-a-lat)*
sweet	***matamis*** *(ma-ta-mis)*
spicy	***maanghang*** *(ma-ang-hang)*

▶ **Is this dish spicy?**
   Maanghang po ba ang putaheng ito?
   (Ma-ang-hang po ba ang pu-ta-heng i-to)

▶ **This dish is too salty.**
   Napaka-alat ng putaheng ito.
   (Na-pa-ka-anlat nang pu-ta-heng i-to)

▶ **That is too spicy for me.**
   Masyadong maanghang iyan para sa akin.
   (Mas-ya-dong ma-ang-hang i-yan pa-ra sa a-kin)

▶ **It's delicious!**
   Ang sarap!
   (Ang sa-rap)

Filipinos usually eat using forks and spoons, although in some high-end restaurants, forks, knives, and spoons are provided. In Chinese, Japanese, and Korean restaurants, chopsticks are provided as well. In precolonial times, and in some areas in the countryside today, some

people used to eat/still eat using their hands, and for
some time in the 1970s and the 1980s this practice was
made popular by some restaurants. Kamayan (literally,
using hands), the restaurant that started this trend,
served grilled food and provided washing areas with
native clay jars with faucets, encouraging people to eat
with their hands.

fork	*tinidor (ti-ni-dór)*
spoon	*kutsara (kut-sa-ra)*
teaspoon	*kutsarita (kut-sa-ri-ta)*
knife	*kutsilyo (kut-sil-yo)*
one more	*isa pa (i-sa pa)*
toothpick	*tutpik (tut-pik)*

► **Please give me a fork.**
   Pahingi po ng tinidor.
   (Pa-hi-ngi po nang ti-ni-dor)

► **Please give me another fork.**
   Pahingi po ng isa pang tinidor.
   (Pa-hi-ngi po nang i-sa pang ti-ni-dor)

► **Can I ask for a knife?**
   Puwede po ba akong makahingi ng kutsilyo?
   (Pu-we-de po ba a-kong ma-ka-hi-ngi nang kut-sil-yo)

► **Do you have toothpicks?**
   May mga tutpik po ba kayo?
   (May ma-nga tut-pik po ba ka-yo)

Rice is the staple food in the Philippines. As such, there are many words for rice: uncooked rice, **bigas**; cooked rice, **kanin**; fried rice, **sinangag**; unhusked grains, **palay**; and crisp/puffed rice, **ampaw**. There is also a variety of wrapped and unwrapped rice cakes. Anything eaten with rice is called "**ulam**."

rice (cooked)	*kanin (ka-nin)*
viand (the main dish that goes with the rice)	*ulam (u-lam)*
chicken	*manok (ma-nók)*
eggs	*itlog (it-lóg)*
fish	*isda (is-dâ)*
beef	*karneng baka (kar-néng ba-ka)*
pork	*karneng baboy (kar-neng ba-boy)*
vegetables	*gulay (gu-lay)*
noodle dish	*pansit (pan-sít)*
broiled	*inihaw (i-ni-haw)*
broiled fish	*inihaw na isda (i-ni-haw na is-dâ)*
whole roasted pig	*lechon (le-chón); litson (lit-són)*

soup	*sopas* (so-pas)
broth	*sabaw* (sa-báw)
dipping sauce	*sawsawan* (saw-sa-wan)
dessert	*panghimagas*
	(pang-hi-ma-gas)
soy sauce	*toyo* (to-yo)
vinegar	*suka* (su-ka)
fish sauce	*patis* (pa-tís)

▶ **Let's start eating.**
Magsimula na po tayong kumain.
(Mag-si-mu-la na po ta-yong ku-ma-in)

▶ **Just a little please.**
Kaunti lang po.
(Ka-un-ti lang po)

▶ **What is the name of this dish?**
Ano po ang pangalan ng putaheng ito?
(A-no po ang pa-nga-lan nang pu-ta-heng i-to)

▶ **What is this dipping sauce?**
Ano po ang sawsawang ito?
(A-no po ang saw-sa-wang i-to)

DRINKS

Among the most popular spots in Metro Manila for
drinks, dancing, and/or live entertainment are: the
Malate area for its restaurants and bars, and Roxas
Boulevard for a view of Manila Bay; Glorietta Mall,
Greenbelt, and Juniper street in Makati, where young
professionals hang out; Bonifacio Global City in
Taguig for its upscale nightclubs; and Tomas Morato
Street, Timog Avenue and Eastwood for restaurants,
bars, comedy clubs and karaoke.

to drink	***uminom*** *(u-mi-nom)*
drink	***inumin*** *(i-nú-min)*
alcoholic drink	***alkohol*** *(al-ko-hól)*
soft drink	***soft drink***
bar	***bar***
bar snacks	***pulutan*** *(pu-lu-tan)*
karaoke bar	***karaoke bar*** (a club with small rooms equipped with karaoke)
clubbing	***mag-clubbing tayo*** *(mag-club-bing ta-yo)*

▶ **What are you doing this evening?**
   Ano ang gagawin mo mamayang gabi?
   (A-no ang ga-ga-win mo ma-ma-yang ga-bi)

► **Let's have a drink.**
Uminom tayo.
(U-mi-nom ta-yo)

► **What would you like to drink?**
Ano'ng gusto mong inumin?
(A-nong gus-tó mong i-nu-mín)

► **Let's go to a club.**
Pumunta tayo sa isang club.
(Pu-mun-ta ta-yo sa isang klab)

► **Let's go to a club where there are women dancing.**
Pumunta tayo sa isang club kung saan may mga babaeng sumasayaw.
(Pu-mun-ta ta-yo sa isang klab kung sa-an may ma-nga ba-ba-eng su-ma-sa-yaw)

► **Can we ask for women to sit at our table?**
Puwede ba kaming mag-imbita ng mga babaeng uupo sa mesa namin?
(Pu-we-de ba ka-ming mag-im-bi-ta ng ma-nga ba-ba-eng u-u-po sa me-sa na-min)

► **What time does the club open/close?**
Anong oras magbubukas/magsasara ang club?
(A-nong o-ras mag-bu-bu-kas/mag-sa-sa-ra ang club)

▶ **What time shall we meet?**
Anong oras tayo magkikita?
(A-nong o-ras ta-yo mag-ki-ki-ta)

▶ **Can I dance with you?**
Puwede bang makipagsayaw sa iyo?
(Pwe-de bang ma-ki-pag-sa-yaw sa i-yo)

water	*tubig (tu-big)*
bottled water	*nakaboteng tubig* *(na-ka-bo-teng tu-big)*
mineral water	*mineral water*
coffee	*kape (ka-pé)*
coffee shop	*kapihan (ka-pi-han)*
tea	*tsaa (tsa-á)*
milk	*gatas (ga-tas)*
lemon	*limon (li-món)*
cocktails	*cocktails*
beer	*beer (bir)* (also called "San Miguel," which is the name of the most popular brand of Philippine beer)
rum	*rum (ram)* (also called "Tanduay," which refers to the most popular brand of Philippine rum)
fermented sugarcane (a local drink)	*tuba (tu-bá)*
rice wine	*tapuy (ta-puy)*

▶ **Water, please.**
   Tubig nga po.
   (Tu-big nga po)

▶ **A cup of coffee, please.**
   Isang tasang kape nga po.
   (I-sang ta-sang ka-pe nga po)

▶ **A bottle of beer, please.**
   Isang bote ng beer nga po.
   (I-sang bo-te nang bir nga po)

▶ **Cheers!**
   Isang tagay! (literally, A toast!)
   (I-sáng ta-gay)

BILLS/RECEIPTS

You may notice that, to ask for the bill, some Filipinos establish eye contact with a waiter, then use both thumbs and index fingers to make a square (the shape of a piece of paper). This means that they would like the bill. Also, should you offer to pay for the bill, most Filipinos will persuade you not to do so and offer to pay instead. Do not simply say "okay." Politely insist, because that sort of "back-and-forth" is usual.

bill/check	*bill/check*
receipt	*resibo (re-si-bo)*

► **Please give me the bill.**
Pahingi na po ng bill/check.
(Pa-hi-ngi na po nang bill/check).

► **Let me pay the bill.**
Ako na ito. (literally, This is me.)
(A-ko na i-to)

Akin na ito. (literally, This is mine.)
(A-kin na i-to)

Ako na. (literally, Me.)
(A-ko na)

► **Please let me pay.**
Sige na, ako na. (literally, Please let me, me.)
(Si-ge na, a-ko na)

► **Can you give me the receipt?**
Pahingi po ng resibo.
(Pa-hi-ngi po nang re-si-bo)

TELEPHONE/CELL PHONE

telephone	*telepono* *(te-le-po-no)*
cell phone	*cell phone* *(sel-fon)*
public phone	*pampublikong telepono* *(pam-pub-li-kong te-le-po-no)*
telephone number	*numero ng telepono* *(nu-me-ro nang te-le-po-no)*
telephone directory	*direktoryo* *(di-rek-tor-yo)*
overseas call	*tawag sa abroad* *(ta-wag sa ab-rod)*
long distance call	*tawag na long distance* *(ta-wag na long distans)*

► **Where is a public phone?**
Saan po mayroong telepono na pampubliko?
(Sa-an po may-ro-ong te-le-po-no na pam-pub-li-ko)

► **I would like to use your phone.**
Gusto ko po sanang makitawag.
(Gus-to ko po sa-nang ma-ki-ta-wag)

► **I want to make a local call.**
Gusto ko pong gumawa ng lokal na tawag.
(Gus-to ko pong gu-ma-wa nang lo-kal na ta-wag)

▶ **I want to make a long-distance call.**
Gusto ko pong mag-long distance.
(Gus-to ko pong mag-long-dis-tans)

▶ **I want to make an overseas call.**
Gusto ko pong tumawag abroad.
(Gus-to ko pong tu-ma-wag ab-rod)

▶ **I want to make a collect call.**
Gusto ko pong tumawag nang collect.
(Gus-to ko pong tu-ma-wag nang ko-lekt)

▶ **May I have your phone number?**
Puwede ko po bang makuha ang numero ninyo sa telepono?
(Pu-we-de ko po bang ma-ku-ha ang nu-me-ro nin-yo sa te-le-po-no)

BUYING A CELLPHONE

Many travelers find that the most cost-efficient way is to just buy either a SIM card (for use on an existing cellphone), or an inexpensive phone in the Philippines and a SIM card. SIM cards and prepaid loads (the amount for such "loads" ranges from 50 to 200 pesos) can be bought not only in shopping malls but also in convenience stores. Texting is relatively cheaper in the Philippines, so many Filipinos prefer this over calling.

store	**tindahan** *(tin-da-han)*
can buy	**makabibili** *(ma-ka-bí-bi-li)*
sell	**nagtitinda** *(nag-ti-tin-da)*

▶ **Where can i buy a cellphone?**
   Saan ako makabibili ng cellphone?
   (Sa-án ako ma-ka-bí-bi-li ng cellphone)

▶ **Do you sell SIM cards?**
   Nagtitinda ba kayo ng SIM card?
   (Nag-ti-tin-da ba ka-yó nang SIM card)

▶ **I would like to buy a SIM card.**
   Pabili ho ng SIM card.
   (Pa-bi-lí ho nang SIM card)

▶ **I would like to buy $200 worth of "load."**
   Pabili ho ng two hundred na "load."
   (Pa-bi-lí ho nang two hundred na load)

▶ **Can I send a text message through your phone?**
   Puwede bang maki-text?
   (Pwe-de bang ma-ki-text)

▶ **I ran out of load.**
   Ubos na ang load ko.
   (U-bós na ang load ko)

▶ **Please text me the information.**
Paki-text sa akin ang impormasyon.
(Paki-text sa a-kin ang im-por-mas-yon)

▶ **I will send you a text message.**
Magte-text ako sa iyo.
(Mag-te-text a-kó sa i-yó)

INTERNET/COMPUTER

internet	*internet (in-ter-net)*
internet café	*internet café (in-ter-net ca-fe)*
computer	*kompyuter (kom-pyu-ter)*
email	*email (e-mãl)* (pronounced as in English)

▶ **I would like to use a computer.**
Gusto ko po sanang gumamit ng kompyuter.
(Gus-to ko po sa-nang gu-ma-mit nang kom-pyu-ter)

▶ **I would like to check my email.**
Gusto ko sanang tingnan ang email ko.
(Gus-to ko sa-nang ting-nan ang e-mail ko)

If you would like to borrow a friend's computer to
check your email, you can use the affix "**maki-**"
(literally, to share).

► **Can I use your computer?**
Puwede bang makigamit ng kompyuter mo?
(Pwe-de bang ma-ki-ga-mit nang kom-pyu-ter mo)

► **Can I check my email on your computer?**
Puwede bang maki-check ng email sa kompyuter mo?
(Pwe-de bang ma-ki-tsek ng e-mail sa kom-pyu-ter mo)

► **What is your email address?**
Ano po ba ang email address ninyo?
(A-no po ba ang e-mail ad-res nin-yo)

USING WI-FI CONNECTIONS

Many shopping malls, coffee shops and restaurants offer free Wifi although internet connections tend to be relatively slower than what you may be used to. Two national programs promote free Wi-fi connections: the Wifi Nation Network initiated by the University of the Philippines National Engineering Center, and the Free Wifi Access Project of the Department of Science and Technology (DOST). Users connect to Wifi Nation Network, log in through Facebook, answer a one-question survery, and then surf the web. Among the public places the DOST project covers are: public plazas and parks;

public primary and secondary central schools; public libraries; rural health units and government hospitals; state universities and colleges; train stations of the MRT and LRT systems; airports and seaports; city and municipal halls; and national government offices. For these public places, there are three levels of access that determine internet speed: first level, 50MB daily data allocation, no assurance of speed, requiring the machine ID of the device; second level, 100MB data allocation, low internet speed, requiring a valid passport for foreigners; and third level, 300MB data allocation, fast internet speed, requiring a government digital certificate.

need	***kailangan*** *(ka-i-la-ngan)*
can connect	***makakokonekta*** *(ma-ka-ko-ko-nek-ta)*

▸ **Do you have Wi-fi here?**
Meron ho bang wifi rito?
(Me-ron ho bang wifi ri-to)

▸ **Where in the mall is there free Wifi?**
Saan ho sa mall merong libreng wifi?
(Sa-án ho sa mall me-rong lib-reng wifi)

▸ **Do you need a password for the Wifi?**
Kailangan ho ba ng password para sa wifi?
(Ka-i-la-ngan ho ba nang password pa-ra sa wifi)

▶ **What is the password for the Wifi?**
Ano ho ang password para sa wifi?
(*A-nó ho ang password pa-ra sa wifi*)

▶ **How can I connect to the internet?**
Paano ho ako makakokonekta sa internet?
(*Pa-a-no ho a-kó ma-ka-ko-ko-nek-ta sa internet*)

SHOPPING

Shopping in the Philippines is usually done in huge shopping malls, and most credit cards are accepted in these establishments. Some department stores are also found within these malls. For fresh fish, meat, and other produce, however, wet markets are popular—and these markets are "wet" because vendors are constantly cleaning the fish stalls. Only cash is accepted in wet markets, but it is common for customers to bargain.

shop	***bili*** *(bi-lí)* (literally, buy)
to shop	***bumili*** *(bu-mi-lí)* (literally, to buy)
shopping	***pamimili*** *(pa-mi-mi-li)*
shopping center	***shopping center*** *(sha-ping sen-ter)*
shopping mall	***shopping mall*** *(sha-ping mol)*

wet market	**palengke** (pa-leng-ke)
price	**presyo** (pres-yo)
receipt	**resibo** (re-si-bo)
drugstore/pharmacy	**botika** (bo-ti-ka)
credit card	**credit card** (kre-dit kard)
souvenirs	**souvenirs/Filipiniana**
	(Fi-li-pin-ya-na)
	(general term that refers to the souvenir section of a department store)

▶ **I want to go shopping.**
Gusto ko pong mamili./
Gusto ko pong mag-shopping.
(Gus-to ko pong ma-mi-li)/
(Gus-to ko pong mag-sha-ping)

▶ **Where is the nearest department store?**
Saan po ang pinakamalapit na department store?
(Sa-an po ang pi-na-ka-ma-la-pit na department store)

▶ **Where is the nearest shopping mall?**
Saan po ang pinakamalapit na shopping mall?
(Sa-an po ang pi-na-ka-ma-la-pit na shopping mall)

► **Where is the nearest wet market?**
Saan po ang pinakamalapit na palengke?
(Sa-an po ang pi-na-ka-ma-la-pit na pa-leng-ke)

► **Is there a souvenir section in this department store?**
May Filipiniana po ba sa department store na ito?
(May Fi-li-pin-ya-na po ba sa department store na i-to)

► **I want to buy this blouse.**
Gusto ko pong bilhin ang blusang ito.
(Gus-to ko pong bil-hín ang blu-sang i-to)

► **I want to buy this ___.**
Gusto ko pong bilhin ang __ na ito.
(Gus-to ko pong bil-hin ang __ na i-to)

► **Please let me buy this medicine.**
Pabili po ng gamot.
(Pa-bi-li po nang ga-mót)

► **Here is my prescription.**
Heto po ang reseta ko.
(He-to po ang re-se-ta ko)

▶ **Please give me a discount.**
Bigyan niyo naman po ako ng tawad.
(Big-yan nyo na-man po a-ko nang ta-wad)

▶ **Is there a discount?**
May tawad ho ba?
(May ta-wad ho ba)

SHOPPING FOR CLOTHES

Tagalog/Filipino has assimilated English words such as *small*, *medium*, and *large* to talk about garment sizes. However, it is good to learn words and phrases you can use when shopping for clothes.

too big	*masyadong malaki*
	(mas-ya-dong ma-la-kí)
too small	*masyadong maliit*
	(mas-ya-dong ma-li-ít)
too wide	*masyadong maluwang*
	(mas-ya-dong ma-lu-wáng)
too tight	*masyadong masikip*
	(mas-ya-dong ma-si-kíp)
fits	*kasya* (kas-ya)
size	*sukat* (su-kat)
same	*pareho/magkapareho*
	(pa-re-ho/mag-ka-pa-re-ho)

different	***iba/magkaiba***	*(ka-i-bá/mag-ka-i-bá)*
color	***kulay***	*(ku-lay)*
design	***di-sen-yo***	*(di-sen-yo)*

► **This is too big.**
Masyadong malaki ito.
(Mas-ya-dong ma-lakí i-to)

► **This is too small.**
Masyadong maliit ito.
(Mas-ya-dong ma-li-ít i-to)

► **This is too wide.**
Masyadong maluwang ito.
(Mas-ya-dong ma-lu-wáng i-to)

► **This is too tight.**
Masyadong masikip ito.
(Mas-ya-dong ma-si-kíp i-to)

► **This fits me.**
Kasya itó sa akin.
(Kas-ya i-to sa a-kin)

► **What is your size?**
Ano ho ang size/sukat nyo?
(A-no ho ang size/sú-kat nyo)

► **I am a Medium.**
Medium ako.
(Medium a-ko)

► **I want a different color.**
Gusto ko ng ibang kulay.
(Gus-tó ko ng i-báng ku-lay)

► **I want the same color.**
Gusto ko ng magkakaparehong ku-lay.
(Gus-tó ko nang mag-ka-ka-pa-re-hong ku-lay)

► **Do you have other designs?**
Meron ba kayong ibang disenyo?
(Me-ron ba ka-yóng i-báng di-sen-yo)

► **I want different designs.**
Gusto ko ng magkakaibang disenyo.
(Gus-tó ko nang mag-ka-ka-i-báng di-sen-yo)

BUSINESS

Although there are business establishments all over
Metro Manila, Makati city is known as the business
center.

business *negosyo (ne-gos-yo)*

occupation	***trabaho*** *(tra-ba-ho)*
business person	***negosyante*** *(ne-gos-yan-te)*
business hours	***oras na bukas*** *(o-ras na bu-kás)*
	(literally, "open hours")

► **What is your business?**
Ano po ang negosyo ninyo?
(A-no po ang ne-gos-yo ninyo)

► **What is your occupation?**
Ano po ang trabaho ninyo?
(A-no po ang tra-ba-ho nin-yo)

► **I am a business person.**
Negosyante po ako.
(Ne-gos-yan-te po a-ko)

► **What are your business hours?**
Anong oras po kayo bukas?
(literally, What time are you open?)
(A-nong o-ras po ka-yo bukás)

POST OFFICE/COURIER COMPANIES

While there are post offices all over Metro Manila, it is sometimes more convenient to send documents or packages through special couriers such as Federal Express

and LBC because they have offices in shopping malls.
Also, a unique-to-the-Philippines phenomenon is the
"**balikbayan** box" (literally, the box of someone who
returns to the country). This term refers to boxes sent
by Filipinos living abroad to their family and friends in
the Philippines where one pays according to the size of
the box and not by weight. Recently, U.S. nationals and
U.S. permanent residents have also been able to use this
service to send boxes from Manila to select cities in the
U.S. English terms are usually used in the post office.

post office	*post office*	*(pos o-pis)*
stamp	*selyo*	*(selyo)*
to send by mail	*ipadala sa pamamagitan ng koreo*	
	(i-pa-da-la sa pa-ma-ma-gi-tan	
	nang ko-re-o)	
letter	*sulat*	*(su-lat)*
envelope	*sobre*	*(sob-re)*
package	*pakete*	*(pa-ke-te)*
documents	*dokumento*	*(do-ku-men-to)*

▶ **I want to send this letter by airmail.**
Gusto ko pong i-airmail ang sulat na ito.
(Gus-to ko pong i-airmail ang su-lat na i-to)

▶ **I want to send this package by Fedex.**
Gusto ko pong ipa-Fedex ang paketeng ito.
(Gus-to ko pong i-pa-Fed-ex ang pa-ke-teng i-to)

▶ **There are documents in this envelope.**
May mga dokumento sa sobreng ito.
(May ma-nga do-ku-men-to sa sob-reng i-to)

▶ **Where can I get this wrapped?**
Saan ko po puwedeng ipabalot ito?
(Sa-an ko po pu-we-deng i-pa-ba-lot i-to)

HEALTH/EMERGENCIES

For many medical conditions, English terms may be used. All medical professionals can easily converse in English. However, should you find yourself traveling in the countryside, it is useful to know some Filipino words to describe your medical condition—as you can easily purchase some over-the-counter medicine in drugstores.

allergy	*allergy*
diarrhea	*diarrhea/pagtatae* (pag-ta-ta-e)

▶ **I have diarrhea.**
Mayroon po akong diarrhea. Nagtatae po ako.
(May-ro-on po a-kong da-ya-ri-ya. Nag-ta-ta-e po a-ko)

cough	***ubo*** *(u-bó)*
runny nose/cold	***sipon*** *(si-pón)*
fever	***lagnat*** *(lag-nát)*
high fever	***mataas na lagnat***
	(ma-ta-as na lag-nát)
headache	***ulo*** *(u-lo)*

▶ **I have a cold.**
May sipon po ako.
(May-si-pon po a-ko)

▶ **I have a fever.**
Nilalagnat po ako.
(Ni-la-lag-nat po a-ko)

▶ **I have a high fever.**
Mataas po ang lagnat ko.
(literally, My fever is high.)
(Ma-ta-as po ang lag-nat ko)

▶ **I have a headache.**
Masakit po ang ulo ko.
(Ma-sa-kít po ang u-lo ko)

▶ **I have a severe headache.**
Masakit na masakit po ang ulo ko.
(Ma-sa-kit na ma-sa-kit po ang u-lo ko)

skin	**balat** *(ba-lát)*
itchy	**makati** *(ma-ka-tí)*
mosquito bites	**kagat ng lamok** *(ka-gát ng la-mók)*
got broken	**nabali** *(na-ba-li)*
leg	**binti** *(bin-tî)*

► My skin is itchy.
   Makati po ang balat ko.
   (Ma-ka-ti po ang ba-lat ko)

► These are mosquito bites.
   Kagat po ng lamok ang mga ito.
   (Ka-gat po nang la-mok ang ma-nga i-to)

► I think my leg is broken.
   Nabali po yata ang binti ko.
   (Na-ba-li po ya-ta ang bin-ti ko)

dentist	**dentista** *(den-tis-ta)*
toothache	**sakit ng ngipin** *(sa-kit nang ngi-pin)*

► I have a toothache.
   Masakit po ang ngipin ko.
   (Ma-sa-kit po ang ngi-pin ko)

► I need to go to a dentist.
   Kailangan ko pong pumunta sa dentista.
   (Ka-i-la-ngan ko pong pu-mun-ta sa den-tis-ta)

sick	***may sakit** (may sa-kít)*
	(literally, have an illness)
patient	***pasyente** (pa-syen-te)*
doctor	***doktor** (dok-tór)*
female doctor	***doktora** (dok-to-ra)*

► **I am sick.**
May sakit po ako.
(May sa-kit po a-ko)

► **I am not feeling well.**
Masama po ang pakiramdam ko.
(literally, I feel bad.)
(Ma-sa-má po ang pa-ki-ram-dam ko)

► **Please send for a doctor.**
Pakitawag po ng doktor.
(Pa-ki-ta-wag po nang dok-tor)

nurse	***nars** (nars)*
hospital	***ospital** (os-pi-tal)*
pharmacy	***botika** (bo-ti-ka);*
	***parmasyotika** (par-mas-yo-ti-ka)*
ambulance	***ambulansiya** (am-bu-lan-sya)*

► **Call an ambulance!**
Tumawag po kayo ng ambulansiya!
(Tu-ma-wag po ka-yo nang am-bu-lan-sya)

▶ **Please hurry up!**
   Bilisan po ninyo!
   (Bi-li-san po nin-yo)

▶ **How far away is the hospital?**
   Gaano kalayo ang ospital?
   (Ga-a-no ka-la-yo ang os-pi-tal)

▶ **The hospital is 20 kilometers away.**
   Dalawampung kilometro ang layo ng ospital.
   (Da-la-wam-pung ki-lo-met-ro ang la-yo nang os-pi-tal)

accident	***aksidente*** *(ak-si-den-te)*
had an injury/got hurt	***nasaktan*** *(na-sak-tan)*
wound, cut	***sugat*** *(su-gat)*

▶ **I met with an accident.**
   Naaksidente po ako.
   (Na-ak-si-den-te po a-ko)

▶ **I got wounded.**
   Nasugatan po ako.
   (Na-su-ga-tan po a-ko)

▶ **I got hurt.**
   Nasaktan po ako.
   (Na-sak-tan po a-ko)

emergency   *emergency (e-mer-gen-si)*

▶ **This is an emergency.**
Emergency po ito.
(E-mer-gen-si po i-to)

▶ **I am disabled.**
May kapansanan po ako.
(May ka-pan-sa-nan po a-ko)

▶ **Is there wheelchair access?**
May daanan po ba para sa mga wheelchair?
(May da-a-nan po ba pa-ra sa ma-nga wheelchair)

▶ **Fire!** (in case of a fire)
Sunog!
(Su-nog)

▶ **Help!** (shout in life-threatening emergencies)
Tulong!
(Tu-lŏng)

▶ **Watch out!** (when danger threatens)
Mag-ingat kayo riyan!
(literally, Please be careful over there!)
(Mag-i-ngat ka-yo dyan)

▶ **Please be careful.**
Mag-ingat po kayo.
(Mag-i-ngat po ka-yo)

▶ **I'm lost.**
Nawawala po ako.
(Na-wa-wa-la po a-ko)

▶ **May I use your telephone?**
Puwede po ba akong makigamit ng telepono?
(Pwe-de po ba a-kong ma-ki-ga-mit nang te-le-po-no)

BARBERSHOP

barber	*barbero* (bar-be-ro)
haircut	*gupit* (gu-pít)
barbershop	*barberya* (bar-ber-ya)

▶ **Is there a barbershop in the hotel?**
May barberya po ba sa hotel?
(May bar-ber-ya po ba sa ho-tel)

▶ **How much for a haircut?**
Magkano po magpagupit?
(literally, How much to have my hair cut?)
(Mag-ka-no po mag-pa-gu-pit)

▶ **Just a trim please.**
 Pakibabawasan lang po nang kaunti.
 (literally, just remove a little bit)
 (Pa-ki-ba-wa-san lang po nang ka-un-ti)

BEAUTY SALON

Many beauty salons in the Metro Manila are one-stop establishments where one can get a haircut, hair coloring, hair styling, a manicure, a pedicure, eyebrow shaping, and even make-up done. Some even offer spa treatments such as massages. In some salons, appointments are not required. Also, in some instances, one can have a manicure, a pedicure, and a hair cut all at once (three people working on you at the same time!).

beauty salon   *beauty parlor; parlor*

▶ **Is there a beauty salon in the hotel?**
 May beauty parlor po ba sa hotel?
 (May beauty parlor po ba sa ho-tel)

have hair styled   *magpa-ayos ng buhok*
                 (mag-pa-ayos nang bu-hók)

▶ **Can I have my hair styled?**
   Puwede po ba akong magpaayos ng buhok?
   (Pwe-de po ba a-kong mag-pa-a-yos nang bu-hok)

▶ **Can I have a blow dry?**
   Puwede po ba akong magpa-blow dry?
   (Pwe-de po ba a-kong mag-pa-blow-dry)

▶ **How much for hair and make-up?**
   Magkano po ang hair at make-up?
   (Mag-ka-no po ang hair at make-up)

▶ **Can I have a manicure and a pedicure at the same time?**
   Puwede po bang sabay ang manicure at pedicure?
   (Pwe-de po bang sa-bay ang manicure at pedicure)

MEASUREMENTS

For measurements, Filipinos are more comfortable with feet, inches, pounds, kilos, and kilometers. Also, it is also common to code-switch (meaning talking in both Filipino and English in a sentence) and give measurements in English but retain the Filipino/Tagalog structure. For example, when asked, a Filipino would usually say "**5'8 at 150 pounds ako.**" (I am 5'8 and 150 pounds.)

height	**taas** *(ta-ás)*
weight	**timbang** *(tim-báng)*
inch	**pulgada** *(pul-ga-da)*
foot	**piye** *(pi-yé)*
kilograms	**kilo** *(ki-lo)*
kilometer	**kilometro** *(ki-lo-met-ro)*

▶ **What is your height?**
   Ano ang taas mo?
   (A-no ang ta-as mo)

▶ **I am five feet ten inches tall.**
   5'10 ako./
   Limang piye at sampung pulgada ako.
   (5'10 a-ko)/
   (Li-mang pi-ye at sam-pung pul-ga-da ako)

▶ **What is your weight?**
   Ano ang timbang mo?
   (A-no ang tim-báng mo)

▶ **I am one hundred and thirty pounds.**
   130 pounds ako./
   Isang daan at tatlumpung libra ako.
   (130 pounds a-ko)/
   (I-sang da-an at tat-lum-pung lib-ra a-ko)

▶ **How far away is the hospital?**
Gaano kalayo ang ospital?
(Ga-a-no ka-la-yo ang os-pi-tal)

▶ **The hospital is 20 kilometers away.**
Dalawampung kilometro ang layo ng ospital.
(Da-la-wam-pung ki-lo-met-ro ang la-yo nang os-pi-tal)

VISITING SOMEONE AT HOME

The most common indigenous Filipino house is the
bahay kubo, which literally means a "cube house"—a
one-room dwelling on stilts made of bamboo and dried
nipa leaves. Philippine architecture reflects the country's colonial history with churches and stone houses
introduced during the Spanish colonial period and
colonial-style government buildings, and "chalets" and
bungalows introduced during the American colonial period and post-war periods.

home (house)	*bahay* (ba-hay)
household	*kabahayan* (ka-ba-ha-yan)
kitchen	*kusina* (ku-si-na)
living room	*sala* (sa-la)
dining room	*komedor* (ko-me-dór)
dinner	*hapunan* (ha-pu-nan)

party	*kasiyahan (ka-si-ya-han);* *party (par-ti)*
bathroom	*banyo (ban-yo)*

► **Thank you for the invitation.**
Salamat po sa pag-imbita ninyo sa akin.
(Sa-la-mat po sa pag-im-bi-ta nin-yo sa a-kin)

► **This looks delicious!**
Mukhang ang sarap po nito.
(Mu-kang ang sa-rap po ni-to)

Usually when offered something, guests make "small talk" by first politely refusing, but when prodded take what is offered. When entertaining in your home, make sure to offer food to your guests twice.

► **Would you like some coffee?**
Gusto niyo po ng kape?
(Gus-to nyo po ba nang ka-pe)

Polite responses are:

► **Please don't bother.**
Huwag na po kayong mag-abala.
(Hu-wag/na po ka-yong mag-a-ba-la)

▶ **It's too much trouble.**
Maaabala pa po kayo.
(Ma-a-a-ba-la pa po ka-yo)

▶ **Please (have some)….**
Sige na po...
(Si-ge na po)

▶ **Okay.**
Sige.
(Si-ge)

▶ **This is delicious.**
Ang sarap!
(Ang sa-rap)

▶ **You cook so well.**
Ang galing po ninyong magluto.
(Ang ga-ling po nin-yong mag-lu-to)

▶ **Thank you for the (very) delicious meal.**
Salamat po sa napakasarap na pagkain.
(Sa-la-mat po sa na-pa-ka-sa-rap na pag-ka-in)

▶ **This party was so much fun.**
Napakasaya po ng party na ito.
(Na-pa-ka-sa-ya po nang par-ty na i-to)

▶ **Thank you for inviting me.**
   Salamat po sa pag-imbita sa akin.
   (Sa-la-mat po sa pag-im-bi-ta sa a-kin)

▶ **Goodbye.**
   Paalam. (formal)
   (Pa-a-lam)

   Sige po. (bye, informal)
   (Si-ge po)

HOLIDAYS

The Philippines has, in general, two kinds of holidays. First, because of the colonial experience and the long struggle for independence, there are many political holidays celebrating, for example, Independence Day, or an important event such as the Fall of Bataan (to the Japanese). Second, because the country is predominantly Christian, Christmas and the Lenten season are official holidays. Moreover, each town (especially in the countryside) has a "patron saint," whose feast day is celebrated with parades, performances, and feasts.

official holiday   *piyesta opisyal*
                              (pyes-ta o-pis-yál)

New Year's Day   *Bagong Taon (Ba-gong ta-on)*
  (January 1)
EDSA anniversary   *anibersaryo ng EDSA*
  (February 25)   *(a-ni-ber-sar-yo nang Ed-sa)*
(From Feb. 22–25, 1986, the Filipinos staged what is
now known as the EDSA [named after the street
Epifanio de los Santos Avenue] revolt to oust former
President Ferdinand Marcos.)

Maundy Thursday   *Huwebes Santo*
  (Hu-we-bes san-to)
Good Friday   *Biyernes Santo*
  (Bi-yer-nes san-to)
  Pasko ng Pagkabuhay
Easter Sunday   *(Pas-ko nang pag-ka-bu-hay)*

Bataan Day   *Araw ng Kagitingan*
  (April 9)   *(A-raw nang ka-gi-ti-ngan)*
(Bataan Day, literally Day of Valor, remembers the Fall
of Bataan to the Japanese soldiers during World War II.)

Labor Day   *Araw ng Manggagawa*
  (May 1)   *(A-raw nang mang-ga-ga-wa)*
Independence Day   *Araw ng Kalayaan*
  (June 12)   *(A-raw nang ka-la-ya-an)*
Ninoy Aquino Day   *Araw ng Kabayanihan ni*
  (August 21)   *Ninoy Aquino*
  (A-raw nang ka-ba-ya-ni-han
  ni Ni-noy A-ki-no)

(Ninoy Aquino was was killed on August 21, 1983, and his death fueled the anti-Marcos movements.)

National Heroes' Day *(August 30)*	***Araw ng mga Bayani*** *(A-raw nang ma-nga ba-ya-ni)*
All Saints's Day *(November 1)*	***Undas/Todos los Santos*** *(Un-dás/To-dos los san-tos)*
Bonifacio Day *(November 30)*	***Kaarawan ni Bonifacio*** *(Ka-a-ra-wan ni Bo-ni-fas-yo)*

(Andres Bonifacio founded the revolutionary organization the Katipunan, which fought for Philippine independence from Spanish rule.)

Christmas Day *(December 25)*	***Pasko***
Rizal Day *(December 30)*	***Araw ng Kabayanihan ni Jose Rizal*** *(A-raw nang ka-ba-ya-ni-han ni Ho-sé Ri-zál)*

(Jose Rizal is the national hero of the Philippines. A medical doctor, he authored two novels which inspired the people to revolt against the Spaniards.)

Last Day of the Year *(December 31)*	***Bisperas ng Bagong Taon*** *(Bis-pe-ras nang ba-gong ta-on)*

SIGHTSEEING

There is no exact translation for the word "sightseeing," because it is not an indigenous concept. However, several Filipino/Tagalog words describe the experience of "going sightseeing."

going sightseeing	***pagsasight-seeing*** *(pag-sa-sight-seeing)*
to take a leisurely stroll/ to go around view	***pamamasyal*** *(pa-ma-mas-yal)* ***tanawin*** *(ta-na-win)*

▶ **I want to go sightseeing.**
   Gusto ko pong magsight-seeing./
   Gusto ko pong mamasyal.
   (Gus-to ko pong mag-sight-seeing)/
   (Gus-to ko pong ma-mas-yal)

Tourist Information Office	***Opisinang Nagbibigay Impormasyon sa mga Turista*** *(O-pi-si-nang Nag-bi-bi-gay Im-por-mas-yon sa ma-nga Tu-ris-ta)*

► **Where is the Tourist Information Office?**
Saan po ang Opisinang Nagbibigay Imporma-syon sa mga Turista?
(Sa-an po ang O-pi-si-nang Nag-bi-bi-gay Im-por-mas-yon sa ma-nga Tu-ris-ta)

► **How far is it from here?**
Gaano po iyon kalayo mula dito?
(Ga-a-no po i-yon ka-la-yo mu-la di-to)

► **How long is the trip?**
Gaano kahaba po ang biyahe?
(Ga-a-no ka-ha-ba po ang bi-ya-he)

POPULAR DESTINATIONS IN METRO MANILA

Most tourist attractions in Metro Manila are known by their English names. However, their names in Filipino/Spanish or other names are provided below.

In recent years, there have been several walking and biking tours of historic places in Manila and sunset cruises at Manila Bay.

Rizal Park

also known as **Luneta** *(Lu-ne-ta)*, an historical park
known for the monument of Jose Rizal, the Philippines' national hero

Manila Bay

baybaying dagat ng Maynila *(bay-ba-ying dagat nang May-nila)* harbor serving Manila's ports;
known for its sunsets

Fort Santiago Intramuros

also known as ***Fuerza de Santiago Intramuros***
(Fu-er-za de San-ti-go In-tra-mu-ros)—walled city
built during the Spanish colonial period

Chinatown

also known as ***Binondo*** *(Bi-non-do)*

National Museum

Pambansang Museo *(Pam-ban-sang Mu-se-o)*—
national history and ethnographty museum

Malacañang Palace

Malakanyang *(Ma-la-kan-yang)*—office and resi-
dence of the Philippine President

Ayala Museum University of the Philippines

Ayala Museum Unibersidad ng Pilipinas *(U-ni-
ber-si-dad nang Pi-li-pi-nas)*

Manila Cathedral

Katedral ng Maynila *(Ka-ted-rál nang May-ni-la)*

Mall of Asia

one of the biggest malls in Asia

Manila Ocean Park
> a marine theme park featuring shows and encounters with sea animals and exhibits

Makati Business District
> leading financial and business district in the Philippines

Bonifacio Global city
> financial district with residential buildings and development projects

POPULAR DESTINATIONS OUTSIDE OF METRO MANILA

Here are brief descriptions of these destinations.

Taal Volcano and Lake
> a volcano within a lake

Tagaytay
> south of Manila with good views of Taal Lake

Baguio
> in northern Luzon; known for its cool climate

Banaue
> north of Baguio; known for its rice terraces

Sagada
> also north of Baguio, known for its caves, hanging coffins and terraces

Ilocos region
   known for its old Spanish architecture

Los Baños
   close to Manila; known for its hot springs

Batangas
   two hours from Manila; known for its beach resorts

Mindoro
   an island reached via a short boat ride from
   Batangas

Boracay island
   a popular island destination; reached by taking a
   plane to Aklan followed by a boat ride

Cebu island
   known for its beach resorts

Davao city
   a short boat ride away is Samal island where Pearl
   Farm is located

Bohol island
   known for its chocolate hills, river tour, and famous
   choir

PART FOUR
Geography Guide & Reading Signs

THE ADMINISTRATIVE REGIONS

The Philippines is divided into three main parts: **Luzon** (the biggest island); **Visayas** (the group of islands in Central Philippines); and **Mindanao** (the second biggest island). It is also further subdivided into regions or administrative divisions. These regions organize the 80 provinces in the country. Except for the Autonomous Region in Muslim Mindanao, these regions do not have separate local governments. Each province is headed by a governor, and each city/town by a mayor.

This list provides you with the name of the region, other names it may be called, or the Tagalog/Filipino name.

National Capital Region/Metro Manila	*Kamaynilaan* (Ka-may-ni-la-an)
Ilocos Region	*Illocos* (I-lo-cos)
Cagayan Valley	*Cagayan* (Ka-ga-yan)
Central Luzon	*Gitnang Luzon* (Git-nang Lu-zon)

CALABARZON	*Cavite, Laguna, Batangas, Rizal, Quezon*
	(Ka-la-bar-zon)
MIMAROPA	*Mindoro, Marinduque, Romblon/Palawan*
	(Mi-ma-ro-pa)
Bikol Region	*Bikol (Bi-kol)*
Western Visayas	*Kanlurang Visayas*
	(Kan-lu-rang Vi-sa-yas)
Central Visayas	*Gitnang Visayas*
	(Git-nang Vi-sa-yas)
Eastern Visayas	*Silangang Visayas*
	(Si-la-ngang Vi-sa-yas)
Zamboanga Peninsula	*Zamboanga*
	(Zam-bwang-ga)
Northern Mindanao	*Hilagang Mindanao*
	(Hi-la-gang Min-da-naw)
Davao Region	*Dabao (Da-baw)*
SOCCSKSARGEN	
Caraga	*(Ka-ra-ga)*
Cordillera	*Kordilyera*
Administrative Region	*(Kor-dil-ye-ra)*

Autonomous Region in Muslim Mindanao

MAJOR CITIES

Manila	***Maynila*** *(May-ni-la)*
Quezon City	***Lungsod ng Quezon***
	(Lung-sod nang ke-zon)
Makati	*(Ma-ka-ti)*
Pasig	*(Pa-sig)*
Marikina	*(Ma-ri-ki-na)*
Parañaque	*(Pa-ra-nya-ke)*
Angeles	*(Ang-he-les)*
Olongapo	*(O-long-ga-po)*
Dagupan	*(Dagupan)*
Baguio	*(Bag-yo)*
Cebu	***Cebu/Sebu*** *(Se-bu)*
Iloilo	*(I-lo-i-lo)*
Bacolod	*(Ba-co-lod)*
Davao	***Dabao*** *(Da-baw)*
Cagayan de Oro	*(Ca-ga-yan de o-ro)*

OTHER KEY WORDS (LAKES, RIVERS, VILLAGES)

region	***rehiyon*** *(re-hyon)*
province	***probinsiya*** *(pro-bin-si-ya)*
city	***lungsod/siyudad***
	(lung-sod/si-yu-dad)
village	***baryo/nayon*** *(bar-yo/na-yon)*
hill	***burol*** *(bu-rol)*

barangay	***barangay*** *(ba-rang-gáy)* *(smallest political unit)*
mountain/s	***bundok/kabundukan*** *(bun-dok/ka-bun-du-kan)*
lake	***lawa*** *(la-wa)*
ocean/s	***karagatan*** *(ka-ra-ga-tan)*
sea	***dagat*** *(da-gat)*
Pacific Ocean	***Karagatang Pasipiko*** *(da-gat pa-si-pi-ko)*
Sulu Sea	***Dagat Sulu*** *(da-gat su-lu)*
Celebes Sea	***Dagat Celebes*** *(da-gat se-le-bes)*
river	***ilog*** *(i-log)*
rural area	***kanayunan*** *(ka-na-yu-nan)*

READING COMMON SIGNS

Some of the signs you will see are in English. However, it is helpful to know some Tagalog/Filipino words in case the signs are written in the native language.

Entrance	***Pasukan*** *(pa-su-kan)*
Exit	***Labasan*** *(la-ba-san)*
Women (for toilets)	***Babae*** *(ba-ba-e)*
Men (for toilets)	***Lalaki*** *(la-la-ki)*
No Smoking	***Bawal Manigarilyo*** *(ba-wal ma-ni-ga-ril-yo)*
Parking Lot	***Paradahan*** *(pa-ra-da-han)*

PART FIVE
Additional Vocabulary

[A]

abroad **ibang bansa** *(i-bang ban-sâ)* (literally, another country)

accident **aksidente** *(ak-si-den-te)*

accommodation (lodging) **matutuluyan/matitirhan** *(ma-tu-tu-lu-yan/ma-ti-tir-han)*

acquaintance **kakilala** *(ka-ki-la-la)*

actor **aktor/artista** *(ak-tór/ar-tis-ta)*

address (location) **tirahan** *(ti-ra-han)* (literally, home address)/**adres** *(ad-rés)*

address (speech) **talumpati** *(ta-lum-pa-ti)*

admission **pagpasok** *(pag-pa-sok)*

admission fee **bayad para sa pagpasok** *(ba-yad pa-ra sa pag-pa-sok)*

admission ticket **tiket para sa pagpasok** *(ti-ket pa-ra sa pag-pa-sok)*

advertisement **patalastas** *(pa-ta-las-tás)*/**adbertisment** *(ad-ber-tis-ment)*

advice **payo** *(pa-yo)*

adviser **tagapayo** *(ta-ga-pa-yo)*

agency **ahensiya** *(a-hen-si-ya)*

agree **payag** *(pa-yag)*

agreement (contract) **kasunduan** *(ka-sun-du-an)*

agriculture **agrikultura** *(ag-ri-kul-tu-ra)*

air force **hukbong panghimpapawid** *(huk-bóng pang-hím-pa-pa-wid)*

alien (foreigner) **dayuhan** *(da-yu-han)*

alley (back street) **eskinita** *(es-ki-ni-ta)*

alphabet **alfabeto** *(al-fa-be-to)*

ambassador **embahador** *(em-ba-ha-dor)*

ambulance **ambulansiya** *(am-bu-lan-si-ya)*

America **Amerika** *(A-me-ri-ka)*

American (person) **Amerikano** *(A-me-ri-ka-no)*

American Embassy **Embahada ng Amerika** *(Em-ba-ha-da nang A-me-ri-ka)*

ancestor **ninuno** *(ni-nu-no)*

ancient **sinauna** *(si-na-u-na)*

animal **hayop** *(ha-yop)*

anniversary **anibersaryo** *(a-ni-ber-sar-yo)*

announcement *pahayag*
(pa-ha-yág)

annual *taunan* (ta-u-nan)

antique *antigo* (an-ti-go)

apology *paumanhin*
(pa-u-man-hin)

appetite *gana* (ga-na)

appetizer *pampagana*
(pam-pa-ga-na)

application *aplikasyon*
(ap-li-kas-yon)

appointment *planong pagkikita*
(pla-nong pag-ki-ki-ta)

approval *pahintulot*
(pa-hin-tu-lot)

architecture *arkitektura*
(ar-ki-tek-tu-ra)

army *hukbong sandatahan*
(huk-bong san-da-ta-han)

arrival *pagdating* (pag-da-ting)

arrive *dating* (da-tíng)

artist *artista* (ar-tis-ta)

Asia *Asya* (As-ya)

Asian *Asyano (As-ya-no)*

assistant *katuwang*
(ka-tu-wang)

association *asosasyon*
(a-so-sas-yon)

athlete *atleta* (at-le-ta)

athlete's foot *alipunga*
(a-li-pu-nga)

Atlantic Ocean *Dagat Atlantiko*
(Da-gat At-lan-ti-ko)

atomic energy *enerhiyang ato-
miko* (e-ner-hi-yang a-to-mi-ko)

attorney *abogado* (a-bo-ga-do)

audience *manonood*
(ma-no-no-od)

auditorium *awditoryum*
(aw-di-tor-yum)

author *awtor* (aw-tor)

automobile *kotse* (kot-se)

award *karangalan* (ka-ra-nga-
lan)

[B]

baby *sanggol* (sang-gol)

bachelor *binata* (bi-na-ta)

bag *bag* (bag)

baggage *bagahe* (ba-ga-he)

bakery *panaderya* (pa-na-
der-ya)

banana *saging* (sa-ging)

bandage *benda* (ben-da)

bank *bangko* (bang-ko)

banquet *handaan* (han-da-an)

bar *bar* (bar)

barber *barbero* (bar-be-ro)

barbershop *barberya* (bar-
ber-yá)

bargain (verb) *tawad* (ta-wad)

barter *palitan ng kalakal*
(pa-li-tan nang ka-la-kal)

bathe (verb) *ligo* (li-go)

bathroom *banyo* (ban-yo);
paliguan (pa-li-gu-an)

batteries *baterya* (ba-ter-ya)

bay *baybaying dagat* (bay)

beach *dalampasigan* (da-lam-
pa-si-gan)

beard *balbas* (bal-bas)

bed *kama* (ka-ma)

bedroom *kuwarto*
(ku-war-to)

beef *karneng baka* (kar-neng
ba-ka)

bellhop **bellman/bellboy**
bicycle **bisikleta** *(bi-sik-le-ta)*
birthday **kaarawan** *(ka-a-ra-wan)*
borrow **hiram** *(hi-ram)*

[C]
cab/taxi **taksi** *(tak-si)*
cabaret **kabaret** *(ka-ba-ret)*
café **kapihan** *(ka-pi-han)*
cake **keyk** *(keyk)*
camera **kamera** *(ka-me-ra)*
camera shop **tindahan ng kamera** *(tin-da-han nang ka-me-ra)*
campus **kampus** *(ka-me-ra)*
cancer **kanser** *(kan-ser)*
candy **kendi** *(ken-di)*
capital (money) **kapital** *(ka-pi-tal)*
capitalism **kapitalismo** *(ka-pi-ta-lis-mo)*
capitalist **kapitalista** *(ka-pi-ta-lis-ta)*
car **kotse** *(kot-se)*
carpenter **karpintero** *(kar-pin-te-ro)*
cashier **kahero** *(ka-he-ro)/* **kahera** *(ka-he-ra)*
catalog **katalogo** *(ka-ta-lo-go)*
centimeter **sentimetro** *(sen-ti-met-ro)*
ceremony **seremonya** *(se-re-mon-ya)*
chair **silya** *(sil-ya)*
change (coins) **barya** *(bar-yá)*
charge (price wanted) **singil** *(si-ngíl)*

charity **kawanggawa** *(ka-wang-ga-wa)*
charming **kaiga-igaya** *(ka-i-ga-i-ga-ya)*
chauffeur **tsuper** *(tsu-pér)/* **drayber** *(dray-ber)*
check (bill) **check** *(chek)*
check (money) **tseke** *(tse-ke)*
check-in **check-in** *(tsek-in)*
child **bata** *(ba-ta)*
children **mga bata** *(ma-nga ba-ta)*
China **Tsina** *(Tsi-na)*
Chinese language **wikang Intsik** *(wi-kang Int-sik)*
Chinese person **Tsino** *(Tsi-no)*
chocolate **tsokolate** *(tso-ko-la-te)*
church **simbahan** *(sim-ba-han)*
claim **pag-angkin** *(pag-ang-kin)*
climate **klima** *(kli-ma)*
clock/watch **relo** *(re-lo)*
cloudy **maulap** *(ma-u-lap)*
coffee shop **kapihan** *(ka-pi-han)*
comb **suklay** *(suk-láy)*
common sense **sentido komun** *(sen-ti-do ku-mon)*
communism **komunismo** *(ko-mu-nis-mo)*
communist **komunista** *(ko-mu-nis-ta)*
company **kumpanya** *(kum-pan-ya)*
competitor **kakumpetensiya** *(ka-kum-pe-ten-si-ya)*
complaint **reklamo** *(rek-la-mo)*
computer **kompyuter** *(kom-pyu-ter)*

conference **kumperensiya**
(kum-pe-ren-si-ya)
confirmation **kumpirmasyon**
(kum-pir-mas-yon)
consent **pagpayag** (pag-pa-yag)
consulate **konsulado**
(kon-su-la-do)
corn **mais** (ma-ís)
crab **alimango** (a-li-ma-ngo)
cup **tasa** (ta-sa)
customer **kostumer** (kos-tu-mer)

[D]
daily **araw-araw** (a-raw-a-raw)
damage **pinsala** (pin-sa-la)
dangerous **mapanganib**
(ma-pa-nga-nib)
date (calendar) **petsa** (pet-sa)
date of birth **araw ng kapanga-
nakan** (a-raw nang ka-pa-nga-
na-kan)
daughter/son **anak** (a-nák)
democracy **demokrasya**
(de-mok-ras-ya)
demonstration **demonstrasyon**
(de-mon-stras-yon)
department **kagawaran**
(ka-ga-wa-ran)
design **disenyo** (di-sen-yo)
dessert **panghimagas**
(pang-hi-ma-gas)
destination **paroroonan**
(pa-ro-ro-o-nan)
dictionary **diksiyonaryo**
(dik-si-yo-nar-yo)
dining room **silid kainan** (si-lid
ka-i-nan)
dentist **dentista** (den-tis-ta)

dirty **marumi** (ma-ru-mi)
discount **diskuwento**
(dis-ku-wen-to)
divorce **diborsiyo** (di-bor-si-yo)
document **dokumento** (do-ku-
men-to)
door **pintuan** (pin-tu-an)
dress **damit** (da-mít)
driver **drayber** (dray-ber)
drugs (medicine) **gamot** (ga-mót)
drugstore **botika** (bo-ti-ka);
parmasyotika (par-mas-yo-
ti-ka)
drunk **lasing** (la-síng)

[E]
ear **tenga** (te-nga)
early **maaga** (ma-a-ga)
early morning **madaling-araw**
(ma-da-ling-a-raw)
earrings **hikaw** (hi-kaw)
earth **daigdig** (da-ig-dig)
mundo (mun-dó)
earthquake **lindol** (lin-dól)
eat out **kumain sa labas**
(ku-ma-in sa la-bás)
economy **ekonomiya**
(e-ko-no-mi-ya)
education **edukasyon**
(e-du-kas-yon)
eggs **itlog** (it-log)
electricity **elektrisidad**
(elek-tri-si-dad)
email **email**
embassy **embahada**
(em-ba-ha-da)
employee **empleado**
(em-ple-ya-do)

engine **makina** (ma-ki-na)
engineer **inhinheyero** (in-hin-ye-ro)
England **Inglatera** (Ing-la-te-ra)
English language **wikang Ingles** (wi-kang Ing-gles)
entrance **pasukan** (pa-su-kan)
envelope **sobre** (sob-re)
Europe **Europa** (Yu-ro-pa)
European **Europeo** (Yu-ro-pe-o)
evening **gabi-gabi** (ga-bí-ga-bí)
every day **araw-araw** (a-raw-a-raw)
evidence **ebidensiya** (e-bi-den-si-ya)
examination (test) **eksamen** (ek-sa-men)
example **halimbawa** (ha-lim-ba-wa)
exchange **palitan** (pa-li-tan)
exchange rate **palitan ng pera** (pa-li-tan nang pe-ra)
executive **eksekyutib** (ek-sek-yu-tib)
exercise **ehersisyo** (e-her-sis-yo)
exhibition **eksibisyon** (ek-si-bis-yon)
exit **labasan** (la-ba-san)
expensive **mahal** (ma-hal)
export **exportasyon** (eks-por-tas-yon)
eye **mata** (ma-tá)

[F]
face **mukha** (mu-ká)
factory **pabrika** (pab-ri-ka)
fake **peke** (pe-ke)
family **pamilya** (pa-mil-ya)

fan **pamaypay** (pa-may-pay)
far **malayo** (ma-la-yo)
fare **pamasahe** (pa-ma-sa-he)
farewell party **despedida** (des-pe-di-da)
farm **bukid** (bu-kid)
favorite place **paboritong lugar** (pa-bo-ri-tong lu-gar)
fee **bayaring halaga** (ba-ya-ríng ha-la-ga)
female **babae** (ba-ba-e)
festival **pista** (pis-tá)
fire (flames) **apoy** (a-póy)
fire (as in "Fire!") **sunog** (su-nog)
fireman **bumbero** (bum-be-ro)
first **una** (u-na)
flag **bandera** (ban-de-ra)
flag, national **bandila** (ban-di-la)
flood **baha** (ba-hâ)
floor **sahig** (sa-hig)
flower **bulaklak** (bu-lak-lak)
flower shop **tindahan ng bulaklak** (tin-da-han nang bu-lak-lak)
folk art **sining bayan** (si-ning ba-yan)
folk songs **awiting bayan** (a-wi-ting ba-yan)
food **pagkain** (pag-ka-in)
foot **paa** (pa-a)
foreigner **dayuhan** (da-yu-han)
forest **gubat** (gu-bat)
fortune teller **manghuhula** (mang-hu-hu-la)
France **Pransiya** (Pran-si-ya)
free (person, country) **malaya** (ma-la-ya)
free (no fee) **libre** (lib-re)

friend **kaibigan** (ka-i-bi-gan)

friendship **pagkakaibigan**
(pag-ka-ka-i-bi-gan)

fruit **prutas** (pru-tas)

full **puno** (pu-nô)

funeral **libing** (li-bing)

furniture **muwebles** (mu-web-les)

future **kinabukasan**
(ki-na-bu-ka-san)

[G]

gamble **sugal** (su-gal)

game **laro** (la-ro)

garage **garahe** (ga-ra-he)

garden **hardin** (har-din)

garlic **bawang** (ba-wang)

gas **gaas** (ga-as)

gasoline **gasolina** (ga-so-li-na)

gas station **gasolinahan**
(ga-so-li-na-han)

gate **tarangkahan**
(ta-rang-ka-han)

gentleman **maginoo** (ma-gi-no-o)

German **Aleman** (A-le-man)

Germany **Alemanya** (A-le-man-ya)

gift **regalo** (re-ga-lo)

girl, young [young teenager]
dalagita (da-la-gi-ta)

glasses (eye) **salamin sa mata**
(sa-la-min sa ma-ta)

gloves **guwantes** (gu-wan-tes)

gold **ginto** (gin-to)

government **gobyerno**
(gob-yer-no)/**pamahalaan**
(pa-ma-ha-la-an)

governor **gobernador**
(go-ber-na-dor)

gram **gramo** (gra-mo)

grandchild **apo** (a-po)

grandfather **lolo** (lo-lo)

grandmother **lola** (lo-la)

guest **bisita** (bi-si-ta)

gun **baril** (ba-ril)

[H]

hair **buhok** (bu-hok)

haircut **gupit** (gu-pit)

hairdresser **taga-gupit at taga-ayos ng buhok** (ta-ga-gu-pit at ta-ga-a-yos nang bu-hok)

harbor **daungan** (da-u-ngan)

harvest **ani** (a-ni)

hat **sumbrero** (sum-bre-ro)

head **ulo** (u-lo)

headache **sakit ng ulo**
(sa-kit nang u-lo)

health **kalusugan** (ka-lu-su-gan)

hear **dinig** (di-nig)

heart **puso** (pu-so)

heavy **mabigat** (ma-bi-gat)

hill **burol** (bu-rol)

historical **makasaysayan**
(ma-ka-say-sa-yan)

history **kasaysayan**
(ka-say-sa-yan)

holiday, public **piyesta opisyal**
(pi-yes-ta o-pis-yal)

homemaker **maybahay**
(may-ba-hay)

honey **honey** (ha-ni); **pukyutan**
(puk-yu-tan)

honeymoon **pulot-gata**
(pu-lot-ga-ta)

hospital **ospital** (os-pi-tal)
hot **mainit** (ma-i-nit)
hour **oras** (o-ras)
house **bahay** (ba-hay)
housework **gawaing-bahay** (ga-wa-ing-ba-hay)
humid **maalinsangan** (ma-a-lin-sa-ngan)
hungry **gutom** (gu-tom)

[I]
ice **yelo** (ye-lo)
ice cream **ice cream** (ays krim)
ill (sick) **may sakit** (may sa-kit)
illegal **ilegal** (i-le-gal)
income **kita** (ki-ta)
industry **industriya** (in-dus-tri-ya)
infant **sanggol**
information desk **information desk**
injection **iniksiyon**
injury **kapansanan** (ka-pan-sa-nan)
insurance **seguro** (se-gu-ro)
interest (money) **interes** (in-te-res)
international **pandaigdigan** (pan-da-ig-di-gan)
internet café **internet café**
interpreter **tagasalin** (ta-ga-sa-lin)
intersection **interseksiyon** (in-ter-sek-si-yon)
introduction **introduction** (in-tro-duk-si-yon)
island **isla** (is-la)

[J]
jacket **dyaket** (dya-ket)
Japan **bansang Hapon** (ban-sang Ha-pon)
Japanese language **wikang Hapones** (wi-kang Ha-po-nes)
Japanese (person) **Hapones** (Ha-po-nes) (male)/**Haponesa** (Ha-po-ne-sa) (female)
jeans, denim **maong** (ma-ong)
jewelry **alahas** (a-la-has)
jewelry store **tindahan nang alahas** (tin-da-han nang a-la-has)
job **trabaho** (tra-ba-ho)
journalist (print) **peryodista** (per-yo-dis-ta)
journalist (general) **mamamahayag** (ma-ma-ma-ha-yag)
journey **paglalakbay** (pag-la-lak-bay)

[K]
karaoke **karaoke** (ka-ra-o-ke)
key **susi** (su-si)
kilogram **kilo** (ki-lo)
kilometer **kilometro** (ki-lo-met-ro)
kiss **halik** (ha-lik)
kitchen **kusina** (ku-si-na)
knife **kutsilyo** (kut-sil-yo)

[L]
late **huli** (hu-lí)
laundry **labada** (la-ba-da)
laundy woman **labandera** (la-ban-de-ra)

law **batas** (ba-tas)

lawyer **abugado** (a-bu-ga-do)

leather **balat** (ba-lat)

lecture **lektura** (lek-tu-ra)

letter **liham** (li-ham); **sulat** (su-lat)

library **aklatan** (ak-la-tan)

license **lisensiya** (li-sen-si-ya)

light **liwanag** (li-wa-nag); **ilaw** (i-law)

lightbulb **bombilya** (bom-bil-ya)

liquor **alak** (a-lak)

literature **panitikan** (pa-ni-ti-kan)

little (amount) **kaunti** (ka-un-ti)

little (size) **maliit** (ma-li-it)

loan **utang** (u-tang)

lock **kandado** (kan-da-do)

lost and found office **opisina para sa nawawalang gamit** (o-pi-si-na pa-ra sa na-wa-wa-lang ga-mit)

luck **suwerte** (su-wer-te)

luggage **bagahe** (ba-ga-he)

lumber **kahoy** (ka-hoy)

lunch **tanghalian** (tang-ha-li-an)

lunch time **oras ng tanghalian** (o-ras nang tang-ha-li-an)

[M]

machine **makina** (ma-ki-na)

maid (domestic worker) **kasambahay** (ka-sam-ba-hay)

margarine **margarina** (mar-ga-ri-na)

magic **salamangka** (sa-la-mang-ka)

mail (send by) **koreo** (ko-re-o)

manager **tagapamahala** (ta-ga-pa-ma-ha-la)

mango **mangga** (mang-ga)

map **mapa** (ma-pa)

market (wet) **palengke** (pa-leng-ke)

marriage **pag-aasawa** (pag-a-a-sa-wa)

married **may asawa** (may a-sa-wa)

massage **masahe** (ma-sa-he)

masseur/masseuse **masahista** (ma-sa-his-ta)

math **matematika** (ma-te-ma-ti-ka)

measure **sukat** (su-kat)

mechanic **mekaniko** (me-ka-ni-ko)

medical insurance **segurong medikal** (se-gu-rong me-di-kal)

medicine (study of) **medisina** (me-di-si-na)

meeting **pulong** (pu-long)

message **mensahe** (men-sa-he)

milk **gatas** (ga-tas)

military **militar** (mi-li-tar)

minister **ministro** (mi-nis-tro)

mirror **salamin** (sa-la-min)

missionary **misyonaryo** (mis-yo-nar-yo)

mistake **pagkakamali** (pag-ka-ka-ma-li)

model **modelo** (mo-delo)

modern **moderno** (mo-der-no)

mosque **moske** (mos-ke)

mosquito **lamok** (la-mok)

mosquito coil **katol** (ka-tol)

mother *ina (i-ná)*/*nanay (na-nay)*

mother-in-law/father-in-law *biyenan (bi-ye-nan)*

motorcycle *motorsiklo (mo-tor-sik-lo)*

mountain *bundok (bun-dok)*

movie *pelikula (pe-li-ku-la); sine (si-ne)*

murder *pagpatay (pag-pa-tay)*

museum *museo (mu-se-o)*

music *musika (mu-si-ka)*

musical *musikal (mu-si-kal)*

musician *musikero (mu-si-ke-ro)*

[N]

name *pangalan (pa-nga-lan)*

napkin *napkin (nap-kin)*

nation *bansa (ban-sa)*

national *pambansa (pam-ban-sa)*

nationality *nasyonalidad (nas-yo-na-li-dad)*

new *bago (ba-go)*

newspaper *diyaryo (di-yar-yo)*

night *gabi (ga-bi)*

noisy *maingay (mai-ingay)*

noodle dish *pansit (pan-sit)*

noon *tanghali (tang-ha-li)*

novel *nobela (no-be-la)*

nuclear *nukleyar (nuk-le-yar)*

number *numero (nu-me-ro)*

nurse *nars (nars)*

[O]

occupation *gawain (ga-wai-in)*

ocean *karagatan (ka-ra-ga-tan)*

office *opisina (o-pi-si-na)*

office worker *kawani (ka-wa-ni)*

official *opisyal (o-pis-yal)*

oil *langis (la-ngis)*

opportunity *pagkakataon (pag-ka-ka-ta-on)*

outline *balangkas (ba-lang-kas)*

oyster *talaba (ta-la-ba)*

[P]

Pacific Ocean *Karagatang Pasipiko (Ka-ra-ga-tang Pa-si-pi-ko)*

package *pakete (pa-ke-te)*

pain *sakit (sa-kit)*

painful *masakit (ma-sa-kit)*

palace *palace (pa-las-yo)*

pants *pantalon (pan-ta-lon)*

paper *papel (pa-pel)*

parents *magulang (ma-gu-lang)*

park *parke (par-ke)*

parking lot *paradahan (pa-ra-da-han)*

party *kasiyahan (ka-si-ya-han)*

passenger *pasahero (pa-sa-he-ro)*

passport *pasaporte (pa-sa-por-te)*

payment *bayad (ba-yad)*

peanuts *mani (ma-ni)*

pearls *perlas (per-las)*

pen *pluma (plu-ma)*

people *mga tao (ma-nga ta-o)*

perfume *pabango (pa-ba-ngo)*

permission *pahintulot (pa-hin-tu-lot)*

pharmacy *parmasyotika (par-mas-yo-ti-ka)*

pill **pildoras** (pil-do-ras)

planet **planeta** (pla-ne-ta)

poem **tula** (tu-lâ)

police **pulis** (pu-lis)

popular music **musikang popular** (mu-si-kang po-pu-lar)

population **populasyon** (po-pu-las-yon)

pork **karneng baboy** (kar-neng ba-boy)

port **daungan** (da-u-ngan)

pregnant **nagdadalang-tao** (nag-da-da-lang-tao)

prescription **preskripsiyon** (pres-krip-si-yon)

president **pangulo** (pa-ngu-lo), **presidente** (pre-si-den-te)

price **presyo** (pres-yo)

priest **pari** (pa-ri)

principle **prinsipyo** (prin-sip-yo)

private **pribado** (pri-ba-do)

private room **pribadong kuwarto** (pri-ba-dong ku-war-to)

profession **propesyon** (pro-pes-yon)

professional **propesyonal** (pro-pes-yo-nal)

professor **propesor** (pro-pe-sor)

profit **kita** (ki-ta)

program **programa** (prog-ra-ma)

project **proyekto** (pro-yek-to)

province **probinsiya** (pro-bin-si-ya)

pull **hatak** (ha-tak)

push **tulak** (tu-lak)

[Q]

qualifications **mga kuwalipi-kasyon** (ma-nga kwa-li-pi-kas-yon)

quality **kalidad** (ka-li-dad)

quantity **kantidad** (kan-ti-dad)

question **tanong** (ta-nong)

quickly **mabilisan** (ma-bi-li-san)

quiet **tahimik** (ta-hi-mik)

quit (give up) **umayaw** (u-ma-yaw)

[R]

race **lahi** (la-hi)

radio **radyo** (rad-yo)

railroad tracks **riles ng tren** (ri-les nang tren)

railway station **estasyon ng tren** (es-tas-yon nang tren)

rain **ulan** (u-lan)

raincoat **kapote** (ka-po-te)

rainy season **tag-ulan** (tag-u-lan)

rank **ranggo** (rang-go)

rash **pantal** (pan-tal)

raw (uncooked) **hilaw** (hi-law)

receipt **resibo** (re-si-bo)

region **rehiyon** (re-hi-yon)

relative (kin) **kamag-anak** (ka-mag-a-nak)

religion **relihiyon** (re-li-hi-yon)

rent (house) **upa** (u-pa)

rent (vehicle) **arkila** (ar-ki-la)

reservation **reserbasyon** (re-ser-bas-yon)

reserved seat **reserbadong upuan** (re-ser-ba-dong u-pu-an)

responsibility **tungkulin**
(tung-ku-lin); **responsibilidad**
(res-pon-si-bi-li-dad)
rest **pahinga** (pa-hi-nga)
restaurant **restawran**
(res-taw-ran)
restroom **banyo** (ban-yo)/**kubeta** (ku-be-ta); **C.R.**
rice (cooked) **kanin** (ka-nin)
rice (uncooked) **bigas** (bi-gás)
rice (grains) **palay** (pa-lay)
rice (fried) **sinangag** (si-na-
ngag)
rice wine **tapuy** (ta-puy)
rich **mayaman** (ma-ya-man)
ring **singsing** (sing-sing)
ripe **hinog** (hi-nog)
river **ilog** (i-log)
read **basa** (ba-sa)
romance **romansa** (ro-man-sa)
room **kuwarto** (ku-war-to)
Russia **Rusya** (Rus-ya)
Russian **Ruso** (Ru-so)

[S]
safe (from harm) **ligtas**
(lig-tas)
safe (for valuables) **kaha de
yero** (ka-ha de ye-ro) (literally,
steel box)
salary **sueldo** (su-wel-do)
sandwich **sandwits** (sand-wits)
schedule **is-ked-yul** (is-ked-yul)
scholar **iskolar** (i-ko-lar)
school **eskuwelahan**
(es-ku-we-la-han)
science **agham** (ag-ham);
siyensiya (si-yen-si-ya)

scissors **gunting** (gun-ting)
seashore **dalampasigan**
(da-lam-pa-si-gan)
seasons **panahon** (pa-na-hon)
secretary **sekretarya**
(sek-re-tar-ya)
service **serbisyo** (ser-bis-yo)
sex (gender) **kasarian**
(ka-sa-ri-an)
sex (act) **pagtatalik** (pag-ta-
ta-lik)
sexy **seksi** (sek-si)
ship **barko** (bar-ko)
shirt **polo** (po-lo); **polo shirt**
shopping **pamimili** (pa-mi-
mi-li)
short (length) **maiksi**
(ma-ik-si)
shrimp **hipon** (hi-pon)
signature **pirma** (pir-ma)
silk **sutla** (sut-la)
singer **mang-aawit** (mang-aawit)
single (not married) **walang
asawa** (wa-lang a-sa-wa)
single man **binata** (bi-na-ta)
single woman **dalaga** (da-la-
ga)
single room **kuwartong pang-
isahan** (ku-war-tong pang-i-
sa-han)
size (fit) **sukat** (su-kat)
sleep **tulog** (tu-log)
smoking **paninigarilyo**
(pa-ni-ni-ga-ril-yo)
snack **meryenda** (mer-yen-da);
minindal (mi-nin-dal)
soldier **sundalo** (sun-da-lo)

snow **niyebe** *(ni-ye-be)*

speaker (person) **tagapagsalita** *(ta-ga-pag-sa-li-ta)*

spicy **maanghang** *(ma-ang-hang)*

sprain **bali** *(ba-li)*

stomachache **sakit ng tiyan** *(sa-kit nang ti-yan)*

stop (halt) **tigil** *(ti-gil)*

street **kalye** *(kal-ye)*

student **mag-aaral** *(mag-a-a-ral)*; **estudyante** *(es-tud-yan-te)*

sugar **asukal** *(a-su-kal)*

suggestion **mungkahi** *(mung-ka-hi)*, **suhestiyon** *(su-hes-ti-yon)*

suit (clothing) **amerikana** *(a-me-ri-ka-na)*

sweetheart **kasintahan** *(ka-sin-ta-han)*, **nobyo** *(nobyo)*, **nobya** *(nob-ya)*

symbol **simbolo** *(sim-bo-lo)*, **sagisag** *(sa-gi-sag)*

system **sistema** *(sis-te-ma)*

[T]

table **mesa** *(me-sa)*

tailor **sastre** *(sas-tre)*

tax **buwis** *(bu-wis)*

taxi **taksi** *(tak-si)*

taxi stand **paradahan ng taksi** *(pa-ra-da-han nang tak-si)*

teacher **guro** *(gu-ro)*

television **telebisyon** *(te-le-bis-yon)*

temperature **temperatura** *(tem-pe-ra-tu-ra)*

temple **templo** *(tem-plo)*

test **pagsusulit** *(pag-su-su-lit)*

theater, movie **sinehan** *(si-ne-han)*

theory **teorya** *(te-yor-ya)*

toast (drinking) **tagay** *(ta-gay)*

toothpick **tutpik** *(tut-pik)*

tourist **turista** *(tu-ris-ta)*

traffic **trapiko** *(tra-pi-ko)*

tree **puno** *(pu-no)*

trousers **pantalon** *(pan-ta-lon)*

truck **trak** *(trak)*

trust (believe) **tiwala** *(ti-wa-la)*; **pananalig** *(pa-na-na-lig)*

truth **katotohanan** *(ka-to-to-ha-nan)*

tunnel **lagusan** *(la-gu-san)*

typhoon **bagyo** *(bag-yó)*

[U]

umbrella **payong** *(pa-yong)*

uncle **tiyo** *(ti-yo)*

unfair **hindi makatarungan** *(hin-di ma-ka-ta-ru-ngan)*

uniform **uniporme** *(u-ni-por-me)*

university **unibersidad** *(u-ni-ber-si-dad)*

unripe **hilaw** *(hi-law)*

untrue **hindi totoo** *(hin-di to-to-o)*

U.S.A **Estados Unidos** *(Es-ta-dos U-ni-dos)*

[V]

vacant **bakante** *(ba-kan-te)*

vacant house **bakanteng bahay** *(ba-kan-teng ba-hay)*

vacation **bakasyon** *(ba-kas-yon)*

vaccination **bakuna** *(ba-ku-na)*

valid **may bisa** *(may bi-sa)*
valley **lambak** *(lam-bak)*
value **halaga** *(ha-la-ga)*
vegetable **gulay** *(gu-lay)*
vendor (seller) **tindero** *(tin-de-ro)*/**tindera** *(tin-de-ra)*
veteran **beterano** *(be-te-ra-no)*
view **tanawin** *(ta-na-win)*
village **nayon** *(na-yon)*
virgin **birhen** *(bir-hen)*
visitor (guest) **bisita** *(bi-si-ta)*
vitamins **bitamina** *(bi-ta-mi-na)*
volcano **bulkan** *(bul-kan)*
voltage **boltahe** *(bol-ta-he)*
vomit **suka** *(su-ka)*
vote **boto** *(bo-to)*

[W]

wage **suweldo** *(su-wel-do)*
wait (for) **hintay** *(hin-tay)*
waiter **weyter** *(wey-ter)*
waitress **weytres** *(wey-tres)*
walk (stroll) **pasyal** *(pas-yal)*
wallet **pitaka** *(pi-ta-ka)*
war **digmaan** *(dig-ma-an)*; **giyera** *(gi-ye-ra)*
watch (timepiece) **relo** *(re-lo)*
waterfall **talon** *(ta-lon)*
watermelon **pakwan** *(pak-wan)*
waves (water) **alon** *(a-lon)*
weapon **sandata** *(san-da-ta)*
weather **panahon** *(pa-na-hon)*
wedding **kasal** *(ka-sal)*
wedding anniversary **anibersaryo ng kasal** *(a-ni-ber-sar-yo nang ka-sal)*
weight **timbang** *(tim-bang)*
west **kanluran** *(kan-lu-ran)*

whale **balyena** *(bal-ye-na)*
wheat **trigo** *(tri-go)*
widow/widower **balo** *(ba-lo)*
win **panalo** *(pa-na-lo)*
wind **hangin** *(ha-ngin)*
window **bintana** *(bin-ta-na)*
windy **mahangin** *(ma-ha-ngin)*
wine **alak** *(a-lak)*
world **mundo** *(mun-do)*; **daigdig** *(da-ig-dig)*
wrap **balot** *(ba-lot)*
wreck **wasak** *(wa-sak)*
write **sulat** *(su-lat)*
wrong **mali** *(ma-lí)*

[X]

x-ray **x-ray** *(x-ray)*

[Y]

yacht **yate** *(ya-te)*
yard **bakuran** *(ba-ku-ran)*
year **taon** *(ta-on)*
young **bata** *(ba-ta)*

[Z]

zoo **zoo** *(zoo)*

About Tuttle
"Books to Span the East and West"

Our core mission at Tuttle Publishing is to create books which bring people together one page at a time. Tuttle was founded in 1832 in the small New England town of Rutland, Vermont (USA). Our fundamental values remain as strong today as they were then—to publish best-in-class books informing the English-speaking world about the countries and peoples of Asia. The world has become a smaller place today and Asia's economic, cultural and political influence has expanded, yet the need for meaningful dialogue and information about this diverse region has never been greater. Since 1948, Tuttle has been a leader in publishing books on the cultures, arts, cuisines, languages and literatures of Asia. Our authors and photographers have won numerous awards and Tuttle has published thousands of books on subjects ranging from martial arts to paper crafts. We welcome you to explore the wealth of information available on Asia at **www.tuttlepublishing.com**.

Published by Tuttle Publishing,
an imprint of Periplus Editions (HK) Ltd.

www.tuttlepublishing.com

Copyright © 2012, 2016 Joi Barrios

Library of Congress Cataloging-in-
Publication Data.

Barrios, Joi.
 Survival Tagalog : how to communicate
without fuss or fear--instantly! / Joi Barrios. -- 1st ed.
    160 p. : 16 cm.
 ISBN 978-0-8048-3942-6 (pbk.)
1. Tagalog language--Conversation
and phrase books--English. 2. Tagalog
language--Spoken Tagalog. I. Title.
PL6055.B379 2012
499'.21183421--dc23

                            2012002071

This edition ISBN 978-0-8048-4559-5

Distributed by:

**North America, Latin
America & Europe**
Tuttle Publishing
364 Innovation Drive
North Clarendon
VT 05759-9436 U.S.A.
Tel: 1 (802) 773-8930
Fax: 1 (802) 773-6993
info@tuttlepublishing.com
www.tuttlepublishing.com

Japan
Tuttle Publishing
Yaekari Building, 3rd Floor
5-4-12 Osaki, Shinagawa-ku,
Tokyo 141 0032
Tel: (81) 3 5437-0171
Fax: (81) 3 5437-0755
sales@tuttle.co.jp
www.tuttle.co.jp

Asia Pacific
Berkeley Books Pte. Ltd.
61 Tai Seng Avenue #02-12,
Singapore 534167
Tel: (65) 6280-1330
Fax: (65) 6280-6290
inquiries@periplus.com.sg
www.periplus.com

20 19 18 17 16
6 5 4 3 2 1   1605CM
Printed in China